Fueling Our Fears

Fueling Our Fears

Stereotyping, Media Coverage, and Public Opinion of Muslim Americans

Brigitte L. Nacos and Oscar Torres-Reyna

ROWMAN & LITTLEFIELD PUBLISHERS, INC.
Lanham • Boulder • New York • Toronto • Plymouth, UK

ROWMAN & LITTLEFIELD PUBLISHERS, INC.

Published in the United States of America
by Rowman & Littlefield Publishers, Inc.
A wholly owned subsidiary of The Rowman & Littlefield Publishing Group, Inc.
4501 Forbes Boulevard, Suite 200, Lanham, Maryland 20706
www.rowmanlittlefield.com

Estover Road, Plymouth PL6 7PY, United Kingdom

Copyright © 2007 by Rowman & Littlefield Publishers, Inc.

British Library Cataloguing in Publication Information Available

Library of Congress Cataloging-in-Publication Data

Nacos, Brigitte Lebens.
  Fueling our fears : stereotyping, media coverage, and public opinion of Muslim
Americans / Brigitte L. Nacos and Oscar Torres-Reyna.
    p. cm.
  Includes bibliographical references and index.
  ISBN-13: 978-0-7425-3983-9 (cloth : alk. paper)
  ISBN-10: 0-7425-3983-0 (cloth : alk. paper)
  ISBN-13: 978-0-7425-3984-6 (pbk. : alk. paper)
  SBN-10: 0-7425-3984-9 (pbk. : alk. paper)
  1. Muslims--United States--Attitudes. 2. Muslims--United States--Public opinion.
3. Muslims--United States--Press coverage. 4. Muslims in popular culture--United
States. 5. Public opinion--United States. 6. United States--Race relations. 7.
United States--Social policy. I. Torres-Reyna, Oscar, 1968- II. Title.
  E184.M88N33 2007
  305.6'970973--dc22

                                                                    2006022151

Printed in the United States of America

♾™ The paper used in this publication meets the minimum requirements of
American National Standard for Information Sciences—Permanence of Paper for
Printed Library Materials, ANSI/NISO Z39.48-1992.

Contents

Acknowledgments

First of all, we owe thanks to Peter Awn, Ester Fuchs, and Reeva Simon, the project administrators, and Louis Abdellatif Cristillo, the project coordinator of the Muslims in New York City Project. After 9/11, Peter, Reeva, and Ester recognized the need to understand how the news media report on the Muslim minority and expanded the project accordingly. Louis managed the lengthy and complex coding process and our team of coders with skill and patience. We are grateful to our excellent coders: Daniel Berghoff, Ayesha Hasan, Seyfi Kenan, Leslie Orderman, Anindita Dutta Roy, and Emilio Spadola.

We are grateful to Pippa Norris, Harvard University; Marion Just, Wellesley College; and Montague Kern, Rutgers University, for inviting us to participate in a colloquium, "Restless Searchlight: Terrorism, the Media, and Public Life," held at the John F. Kennedy School of Government, Harvard University, in August 2002, and for including an earlier version of this volume's chapter 1 in their edited volume *Framing Terrorism: The News Media, Government, and the Public*. We found their and other colloquium participants' thoughtful comments tremendously helpful. Brenda Hadenfeldt at Rowman & Littlefield was interested in this project early on and guided us along the way. We appreciate her guidance and judgment.

Last but not least, we thank the Ford Foundation for funding the media study within the larger Muslims in New York City Project and thus a large part of the research presented in this volume.

Preface

Yesterday I saw first hand how anger over the World Trade Center attacks turns on Muslims who call New York home. At 4:30 p.m. on 116th Street, five black teenagers stopped in front of the American Muslim Community of East Harlem site—a closet-sized candy store with a make-shift mosque in a back room. Tiny store owner Muhammad Chaudhry stood in the doorway. One of the teenage boys asked him, "Do you feel sorry for America?" The kid gave Chaudhry a knock-out punch in the face that sent him reeling backwards and onto the floor. Blood spurted all over his plaid shirt, the linoleum floor and a pair of sneakers left by a man who was praying. Chaudhry's dentures cracked in two.

In Huntington, L.I., a 75-year-old drunk man tried to run over a Pakistani woman at a shopping mall and threatened to kill her for "destroying my country." In Chicago a Molotov cocktail was tossed at a Muslim community center.

—J. K. Dineen reporting in the *New York Daily News* on Sept. 14, 2001

And then there are some of the postings on our ABC News message board: "The Muslims are a bunch of savages that should be nuked off the face of the earth." "The Islamic way of life, their nations, their culture must be eradicated." "We should deport them and make it illegal for Arabs to live here until terrorism is completely eliminated."

—*World News Tonight* (ABC News) on September 12, 2001

Accounts like the ones excerpted above were plentiful in the immediate aftermath of the attacks on the World Trade Center and the Pentagon. While they were disconcerting, these reports also showed that the news media, in spite of being overwhelmed by the news about the horrific events of 9/11, did not ignore the fact that Muslim and Arab Americans became the targets of a backlash of anger and thirst for revenge. Indeed, in the three days following the terror strikes, a total of 268 newspaper articles and wire service dispatches reported about outright attacks and threats against Muslims and Arabs across the nation, fears in Muslim communities around the country, and appeals against anti-Muslim bigotry by President George W. Bush and other leaders. ABC News, CBS News, NBC News, and CNN aired a total of sixteen news segments that dealt with the predicament of Muslims and Arabs in post-9/11 America. But these reports also raised questions: Why were many Americans ill informed about Muslims in the United States? Why were Muslim and Arab Americans suspected of being or sympathizing with terrorists? According to American Muslim leaders, the threats against fellow Muslims came "from people who are ignorant of the Muslim faith" and "falsely assume that all Muslims are fundamentalist extremists." To what extent and how did the U.S. media report on Muslim communities before the attacks of 9/11 and play a role in informing and educating the American public about this minority—or fail to do so? Moreover, how did the news media portray Muslims across the United States in the months following the immediate aftermath of 9/11—another possible factor in influencing how the non-Muslim majority in America feels about Muslims at home and abroad?

We got an opportunity to examine these questions and many others thanks to the farsightedness and initiative of Peter Awn, Reeva Simon, and Ester Fuchs, project administrators and principal investigators of the Muslims in New York City project at Columbia University. Commenced in 1998 and generously funded by the Ford Foundation, the project aimed at exploring in an interdisciplinary fashion questions of identity, social and cultural accommodation, economic participation, and political engagement as they relate to Muslims' individual and collective experiences in New York City. Initially, the project did not include research of the media's portrayal of New York's Muslims. But shortly after 9/11, the project administrators recognized the value of examining pertinent news coverage in the post-9/11 climate and got Brigitte Nacos involved as investigator of the new media study. Nacos, in turn, brought Oscar Torres-Reyna aboard for his expertise in statistical analysis.

Although originally conceived as a study of the New York media's post-9/11 reporting on Muslims in New York, our research expanded to national media and news about Muslims in the national setting before and after 9/11 and, in a more limited scope, to the news treatment of Muslims abroad. In today's global and instant media and communications landscape, local, domestic, and international reporting affects readers, listeners, and viewers in near and faraway places. The controversy following the publication of cartoons that depicted the Prophet Muhammad as a terrorist was a case in point. What editors of the Danish newspaper that first published the cartoons regarded as the exercise of their freedom of expression and Muslims as the most blatant kind of blasphemy wouldn't have grown into a major international crisis in early 2006 without the global media's massive coverage. As the global coverage of the controversy intensified and more Internet sites allowed viewers everywhere to see the cartoon images, angry anti-Danish and anti-Western protests spread like fire through the Muslim world.

The first three chapters of this volume are in large part the result of the media research we conducted within the Muslims in New York City project; the first part of the last chapter makes extensive use of the transcripts from twenty-five focus group sessions with American Muslims that were conducted by other researchers in the Muslims in New York City project. The focus group participants were of various backgrounds in terms of age, gender, race, ethnicity, and profession. We conducted additional research, especially for chapters 4 and 5, in addition to our work within the Muslims in New York City project. The great diversity of participants in these focus groups was indicative of the range of ethnic, racial, and religious backgrounds of Muslims in America. Thus, while we examined media, public opinion, and other areas as they related to this minority and while we write about Muslim Americans as if they constituted a monolithic group, in reality there are many distinctions. For example, there are Sunnis and Shiites, Muslims born in the United States, and others who come from various parts of Asia, Africa, Europe, and Latin America.

Chapter 1 is based on the systematic content analyses of many hundreds of print and television news items related to Muslims in the New York metropolitan area, in the United States, and abroad during the months before and after 9/11. The quantitative and qualitative examination of written and spoken words resulted in the surprising finding that the pertinent coverage actually improved in the immediate post-9/11 period in several respects, including an increase in the use of Muslim sources, a switch from mostly episodic to mostly thematic reporting, and an overall more positive portrayal of Muslims.

But because we wondered whether these positive changes were just temporary or harbingers of lasting improvements, we also analyzed all pertinent news several weeks before and after the first 9/11 anniversary in the same media. This examination and additional research revealed that the news around the first anniversary—and beyond—moved back toward the pre-9/11 coverage patterns. Chapter 2 demonstrates that imbalances in reporting on Muslims in America are not inevitable, by describing one newspaper's exemplary reporting on American Muslims and their religion.

Whether or not a picture—or better, the meaning of a picture—is worth a thousand words, there is little doubt that visuals make more memorable impressions on those who see them and, just as important, create new stereotypes and reinforce traditional stereotypes. Our analysis of pre- and post-9/11 images of Muslims and Arabs at home and abroad demonstrated bias in favor of stereotypical depictions of both male and female Muslims and Arabs (chapter 3).

Chapter 4 examines the American public's attitudes toward American Muslims, Muslims abroad, and Islam. While many Americans hadn't heard enough about Muslims and Islam before 9/11 to form opinions on Muslims and their religion, far more revealed pertinent attitudes after the attacks in New York and Washington. One of the more striking findings of opinion research was that heavy news consumers were far more fearful of additional terrorist strikes and far more willing to accept the abridgment of American Muslims' civil liberties than were light news consumers.

How the news media dealt with the controversial issue of torturing captured terrorists and suspected terrorists is the topic of chapter 5. Since most, if not all, of the detainees in the "war on terrorism" were, and still are, Muslims and/or Arabs, we felt that the media's treatment of the torture debate was a fitting topic for this volume. We found that the advocates of torture for the sake of preventing counterterrorism were the dominant voices in the news before the revelation of the Abu Ghraib torture scandal. Thereafter, news organizations displayed great reluctance to use the word "torture" in their coverage of even the most brutal treatment of detainees unless the term was actually used by authoritative sources they could cite—particularly administration officials who denied that Americans tortured or outsourced torture to foreign governments. As we mentioned before, what happens in faraway places to members of ethnic, racial, or religious groups affects news consumers everywhere. And in this case, the images of Abu Ghraib were seen by people around the world, including Americans, Muslims and non-Muslims alike.

In chapter 6, we first explore Muslim Americans' views about the American media, their assessment of the media's influence on the U.S. public, and their minority's chances of getting heard and seen in the news. Secondly, based on survey data, we examine the Muslim minority's attitudes toward non-Muslim Americans and, just as important, toward post-9/11 U.S. counterterrorist policies and practices, such as the profiling of "Middle Easterners" and the "war on terrorism" abroad.

1

Muslim Americans in the News before and after 9/11

When a powerful bomb destroyed the Alfred P. Murrah Federal Building in Oklahoma City on April 19, 1995, news organizations were quick to identify Middle Easterners as suspects and reported that the FBI was specifically looking for two men with dark hair and beards. Within hours, Arab and Muslim Americans became the targets of physical and verbal assaults. As it turned out, an American with European ancestors, Timothy McVeigh, committed what was said at the time to be the most deadly terrorist deed on American soil. When the twin towers of the World Trade Center crumbled into a nuclear-winter-like cityscape and part of the Pentagon outside of Washington, DC, went up in flames on September 11, 2001, news organizations reported soon thereafter, this time correctly, that the perpetrators were Arabs and Muslims. And once again, perfectly peaceful Arab and Muslim Americans as well as persons "looking like them" became the victims of hate crimes and of the stereotypical image of Muslims and Arabs as perpetrators of violence and terrorists.

The preponderant use of cliches to characterize and demonize Muslims and Arabs has been perceived for a long time by some observers and documented well by others.[1] "The reason why many Arab and Muslim Americans are discriminated [against]," wrote one Amazon.com customer-reviewer shortly after the events of 9/11, "is because many people probably think of the 'TV-Arab' image (i.e., suicide bomber, fanatics, lazy, etc.)."[2] Although Hollywood movies, television shows, and popular fiction have long dwelled on stereotypical portrayals of Arabs and Muslims, one would not necessarily expect similar typecasting and cliches in the news. However, popular culture and news reporting do not operate in a vacuum but seem to feed on each other. Discussing the depiction of Middle Easterners in crime fiction, Reeva Simon concluded that "authors know that today, after watching the evening news and reports of bombed American embassies, kidnapped or killed diplomats, and the latest exploits of religious fanatics, the public will readily read about Middle Eastern conspirators and that books about the area will sell."[3]

Years ago, with the Iranian hostage crisis fresh in mind, Edward Said wrote about the failure of the American media and U.S. experts to understand and explain the Arab and Muslim world. In particular, he argued that "Muslims and Arabs are essentially covered, discussed, apprehended either as suppliers of oil or as potential terrorists. Very little of the detail, the human density, the passion of Arab-Muslim life has entered the awareness of even those people whose profession it is to report the Islamic world."[4]

Muslim Americans have long been convinced that the news about them is colored by negative biases. This was clearly expressed by Muslim New Yorkers who participated in focus groups well before the events of 9/11. Muslim women especially mentioned the media's tendency to stereotype Muslim males as violent and Muslim women as submissive.[5] This belief among American Muslims and Arabs in a widespread anti-Muslim news slant did not weaken after 9/11. On the contrary, less than a month after the attacks of 9/11, teenage students in a Muslim school in Brooklyn, for example, expressed the conviction that "Muslims are the victims of a prejudiced news media. As one sixteen-year-old girl put it, "[a] lot of newspapers write negative things, and we get so upset."[6] In the spring and summer of 2002, some Arab merchants in Brooklyn tried to organize a boycott of the *New York Post* to dramatize their opposition to what they believed was an anti-Arab and anti-Muslim stance and the tabloid's consistently pro-Jewish/pro-Israel coverage. The goal was to convince Arab-American merchants to keep the *Post* off their newspaper shelves. According to flyers in English and Arabic that were distributed to vendors, the *New York Post* "is not only pro-Zionist, but it hates everything called Islamic or Arabic."[7]

Complaints about negative mass-mediated stereotypes before and after September 11, 2001, were not peculiar to Muslims in New York City, but were shared by Muslims across the United States. According to the American Muslim Poll that questioned Muslims in the United States in October and November 2001, more than two in three (68 percent) respondents said that the news media were not fair in their portrayal of Muslims and Islam (better than three of four or 77 percent thought that Hollywood was not fair in this respect).[8] This chapter examines how major American news organizations have reported on Muslim Americans. We were particularly interested in answering the following questions:

1. Was the portrayal of Muslim Americans in the news mostly negative and stereotypical?

2. Did the events of 9/11 alter the coverage of the Muslim American minority and if so, how did these changes manifest themselves?
3. Did the pertinent news coverage of New York City and neighboring counties with rather large Muslim populations differ from the national coverage?

THE NEWS AND THE "PICTURES IN OUR HEADS"

Some eighty years ago, before the advent of radio and television, Walter Lippmann observed that what people know about the world around them is mostly the result of secondhand knowledge received through the press and that the "pictures in our heads" are the result of a pseudoreality reflected in the news.[9] In modern-day mass societies people are even more dependent on the news because they have "nowhere else to turn for information about public affairs and for cues on how to frame and interpret that information."[10]

The media tend to report the news along explanatory frames that cue the reader, listener, and viewer to put events, issues, and political actors into contextual frameworks of reference.[11] Framing can and does affect the news in many ways, for example, in the choice of topics, sources, language, and photographs. According to Robert Entman, "a frame operates to select and highlight some features of reality and obscure others in a way that tells a consistent story about problems, their causes, moral implications, and remedies."[12] Accordingly, reporters, editors, producers, and others in the news media constantly make decisions as to what and whom to present in the news and how. These choices are influenced by news organizations' standard operating procedures. W. Lance Bennett, for example, suggests that "sources and viewpoints are 'indexed' (admitted through the news gates) according to the magnitude and content of conflicts among key government decision-makers or other players with the power (as perceived by journalistic insiders) to affect the development of a story."[13] Whether the press covers the critical voices and viewpoints of more or less established interests depends on the particular positions of authoritative sources, especially government insiders. Because "indexing" has proven to be most potent in foreign news, one wonders whether it affects the coverage of Muslim Americans in the face of the perennial "Middle East problem" between Israelis and Palestinians and the United States government's traditional support for Israel. It has been suggested that foreign news "has two dimensions: the foreign story that deals with events abroad and the domestic story that concentrates on the United States' role and reaction to world events."[14] Similarly, domestic coverage may have two dimensions as well: one that concentrates on ethnic and religious minorities in America (i.e., Muslim and Arab Americans) and another that concentrates on their ties to their regions of origin (i.e., the Middle East).

Some framing patterns seem especially important in terrorism news and the perceptions and reaction of news consumers. Shanto Iyengar found that TV network coverage of terrorism in the 1980s was overwhelmingly episodic or narrowly focused rather than thematic or contextual. His research demonstrated that narrowly focused coverage influenced audiences to hold the individual perpetrators responsible, while thematic reporting was more likely to assign responsibility to societal conditions and public policies. Moreover, when exposed to episodic framing of terrorism, people were more inclined to support punitive measures against individuals; when watching thematically framed terrorism news, audience members tended to be more in favor of policies that deal with and even remove the root causes of terror.[15]

OF STEREOTYPES AND "SYMBOL HANDLERS"

We know more of the portrayal of African Americans in the news than about the coverage patterns with respect to other minorities. Research has pointed to one persistent problem in the way the news reports about black Americans, namely the tendency to highlight the extraordinary at the expense of what is the routine of everyday life in black communities. As a result, nonblack Americans—especially whites—think of black America in terms of stereotypes—positive in regard to African American superstars in sports and entertainment and negative as to black males as criminals and black females as welfare queens.[16] Researchers found that few whites are aware of this hero-or-villain syndrome that seems especially prevalent in TV news.[17]

It seems that reporting on other minorities is equally spotty and stereotypical. With respect to Latinos in the United States, for example, one study found that in six southwestern cities the media mostly covered Hispanics in the context of sports and otherwise in terms of soft news (Greenberg 1986). Another study established that in regions with sizable Mexican American populations few reports were exclusively or primarily about the Mexican American minorities.[18] And the report of President Clinton's Advisory Board on Race noted under the heading "Media and Stereotyping" that apart from African Americans "a major problem still remains regarding the representation, coverage, and portrayal of minorities on the news." One board member, former New Jersey governor Thomas Kean, reported that "[a]lmost every group we have gone to has said that the media is a problem that has to be addressed."[19] Presumably, Muslim Americans represented one of those groups.

By framing the news along the lines of the traditional attitudes and prejudices of society's predominant groups, the news media convey stereotypes that affect a broad range of public perceptions, among them how people think about race, ethnicity, and religion. According to Todd Gitlin media frames are "persistent patterns. . . , by which symbol handlers routinely organize discourse, whether verbal or visual."[20] "Symbol handlers" are still most and foremost members of the white majority and their news judgments are increasingly affected by the profit imperatives of the large media corporations, but day-to-day decisions in the newsrooms are also influenced by deep-seated prejudices in the dominant white Western culture. A generation ago, Herbert Gans found that "the news reflects the white male social order."[21] While contemporary newsrooms are more diverse than twenty-five years ago, entrenched prejudices and stereotypical perceptions have not disappeared. One experienced newsman observed recently that "Newsrooms are not hermetically sealed against the prejudices that play perniciously just beneath the surface of American life."[22] And according to another expert in the field, "Journalism helps shape how racially diverse people think of each other and how public policy on race-related issues is formulated."[23] It seems equally true that the media affect how religiously diverse people view each other. Referring to the predominant visual images of black Americans in the media's depiction of poverty in America, Martin Gilens concluded that "subconscious stereotypes" guide newsroom decisions.[24] Similarly, overtly rejected stereotypes may nevertheless affect subconsciously the judgments concerning the news about American Muslims and Arabs.[25]

Given the persistent complaints about media bias by American Muslims and their organizations and the growth of this minority, our research aimed at shedding light on the way the news media report on Muslim Americans in New York City and across the United States.[26] Since the U.S. government is prohibited from collecting census data on people's religious affiliations, there are no official data on the total number of Muslims in the United States. Estimates range from one to seven million—with the real number somewhere in the middle—and, according to Muslim organizations, closer to the higher end of these assumptions.[27] According to a recent religious survey, the proportion of Muslims in the U.S. population may be 1 percent, but experts among American Muslims believe 2 percent to be more realistic.[28] As for New York City, researchers at Columbia University, who canvassed the city's five boroughs to locate Muslims and their communities, have estimated that a total of about six hundred thousand Muslims live in these areas.[29] Assuming that this is a sound number and considering that New York City has a total population of just over eight million according to the 2000 census, Muslims represent about 7.5 percent of the city's population and thus a sizable religious minority.

We are aware that not all Arabs in the United States (or abroad) are Muslims and that probably only about one in four Arab Americans are

6 — *Chapter 1*

Muslims. We have nevertheless included Arab Americans in this study because as the news media report on Muslims and Arabs at home and abroad, they frequently seem to use the terms as if they were interchangeable.

The stereotypes that depict Muslims and Arabs as perpetrators of violence and terrorism were magnified by a long series of spectacular anti-American acts of terror that extended from the long-lasting Iranian hostage crisis (1979–81) to the suicide attack on the USS *Cole* in 2000. All of these incidents in the 1980s and 1990s (including the first World Trade Center bombing in 1993) were widely reported, indeed overreported, as the news media dwelt on shocking images of death, destruction, and the victims of this sort of political violence.[30] But because none of the previous strikes came even close to what happened on September 11, 2001, there was reason to investigate whether this unprecedented event triggered changes in the news with respect to American Muslims.

SELECTION OF LOCAL AND NATIONAL NEWS MEDIA

For our newspaper analysis we selected the three largest daily newspapers that are published in New York City, the *New York Times, New York Post,* and *Daily News*. While the *Times* has a sizable national circulation besides its local and regional readership and a reputation as an influential local, regional, and national news organ (and a leading international news source as well), the *Post* and the *Daily News* are mostly read in the New York metropolitan area. Additionally, we chose *USA Today* because of its national focus and readership. We also examined the transcripts of pertinent stories televised by CBS News on *The Early Show* and the *Evening News with Dan Rather*. (For a detailed description of our research methodology, see the appendix.) Since earlier research has demonstrated that the news broadcasts of the major TV networks have very similar content, we restricted our analysis to only one of the TV networks.[31]

9/11 AND THE NEWS ABOUT AMERICAN MUSLIMS

It came hardly as a surprise that we found significantly more news that reported about or mentioned Muslim Americans and Arab Americans in the post-9/11 period than in the months preceding the attacks. We did not, however, expect to find that the four newspapers combined published nearly eleven times as many relevant stories in the six months after 9/11 as in the six months before and three times as many as in the twelve months before the terror attacks.

Table 1.1 Muslim and Arab Americans in the News before and after 9/11

	Sept. 11, 2000, to March 11, 2001 (6 months)	March 12, 2001, to Sept. 11, 2001 (6 months)	Sept. 12, 2001, to March 11, 2002 (6 months)
	(N)	(N)	(N)
New York Times	37	17	376
New York Post	58	15	50
Daily News (NY)	52	21	99
USA Today	8	6	128
Total:	155	59	653

N = Number of stories
Source: Muslims in New York City Project

Each of the four publications reported far more frequently on Muslim and Arab Americans in the six months after than in the six months before the terror attacks. At first sight, however, it seemed surprising that the *New York Post*, unlike the *New York Times* and *USA Today*, published more stories with references to Muslim and Arab Americans in the twelve months before than in the six months after 9/11 and that there was only a modest increase in pertinent news in the *Daily News* (see table 1.1). This was the result of these tabloids' extensive reporting on campaign donations that then–First Lady Hillary Clinton had received from American Muslim organizations in her New York race for the U.S. Senate in the fall of 2000, and their spacious coverage of controversial issues raised about the endorsement of candidates by Muslim groups during New York City's municipal primaries in the summer of 2001 and of similar partisan disputes in the New York metropolitan area. Still, the comparison of the six months before and after 9/11 leaves no doubt about the increased frequency of stories on American Muslims and Arabs in all four newspapers after the terrorist attacks. According to one observer, this was no coincidence but the result of the news media's efforts in "reaching out to Muslim civic leaders, visiting mosques, and in general providing opportunities to American Muslims to 'speak their minds.'"[32]

Just as news organizations paid far more attention to American Muslims and Arabs following the terror of 9/11, they covered Muslims, Arabs, and Islam in general far more frequently as well (see table 1.2). One comprehensive content analysis of religious news in ten American daily newspapers, nine newsmagazines, and one wire service (the Associated Press) found that stories on Islam and Muslims dominated this coverage in the weeks following the events of 9/11. Indeed, 70 percent of the stories fully devoted to religion concerned Islam and Muslims and

Table 1.2 Muslims, Arabs, and Islam in the News before and after 9/11

	Muslim Period I	Muslim Period II	Arab Period I	Arab Period II	Islam Period I	Islam Period II
	(N)	(N)	(N)	(N)	(N)	(N)
ABC News	31	163	11	99	1	31
CBS News	32	144	27	117	1	27
NBC News	9	98	5	90	—	18
CNN	23	203	43	200	1	31
Fox News	1	100	2	64	1	46
NY Times	345	1,468	345	1,272	216	1,190
NPR	54	217	53	182	10	84

N = Number of news segments/articles mentioning the search words Muslim, Arab, and/or Islam. Period I = 6 months before the terrorist attacks of September 11, 2001; Period II = 6 months after the attacks of 9/11.
Source: Muslims in New York City Project

the remaining 30 percent dealt with Christianity and Christians, multifaith and nondenominational persons, Judaism and Jews, and Buddhism and Buddhists.[33] This surge was a natural reaction to the attacks that killed more than three thousand Americans and were perpetrated by Muslim and Arab followers of America's most wanted terrorist leader, Osama bin Laden. In the process, Americans learned a great deal about the Muslims in their midst and their religion. On the other hand, the sudden media attention to the Muslim and Arab world and the religion of Islam also happened to satisfy terrorists' perennial need for publicity.[34]

Muslim and Arab Americans rarely made the front pages before 9/11. Indeed, in the six months before 9/11, none of the newspapers carried a story about Muslim Americans on its front page. In the six months following September 11, the *New York Times* placed one of ten news stories that were about or mentioned Muslim or Arab Americans on the front page; the ratio was somewhat smaller in *USA Today* (7 percent) and much smaller in *New York Post* and the *Daily News*.

While in all four newspapers the number of articles that covered, mentioned, or quoted American Muslims and American Arabs increased after 9/11, there was otherwise no uniformity: The *Times* and *Daily News* presented their readers with significantly more news analyses, the *Post* and *USA Today* carried a larger proportion of opinion columns that addressed one or the other aspect of American Muslims and Arabs, and *USA Today* published more pertinent letters-to-the-editor and more editorials. Taken together, the newspapers devoted a significantly larger proportion of their total news about American Muslims to analytical perspectives, elite opinion, and the sentiments of readers at a time when the American public needed to be informed and educated about fellow Americans who happened to be Muslims.

MUSLIM AMERICAN VOICES IN THE NEWS

TV correspondents who cover presidential election campaigns amass significantly more airtime than the candidates themselves, a situation also common in television news in general. The print media, too, rely a great deal on journalistic descriptions and background information.[35] In the months before 9/11, a date some have come to call "Black Tuesday," one in five sources that provided descriptions or background information were journalists, reporters, and correspondents, but in the six months thereafter, editors and perhaps reporters themselves seemed less inclined to rely on journalistic explanations and were more open to letting Muslim and Arab Americans express their views and sentiments. As a result, in the half a year after 9/11, four of ten sources quoted in articles about Muslim or Arab Americans were Muslim and Arab citizens or residents compared to one-third in the previous six months and only one-fourth in the previous year. All three New York newspapers used these sources more frequently after "Black Tuesday" than in the year before. The increase was especially striking in the *Times* in that the share of Muslim American and Arab American sources increased from about one-fourth in the year before 9/11 to nearly one-half afterwards. The exception was *USA Today*, where the share of Muslim and Arab American sources actually declined slightly from nearly one-third before 9/11 to slightly more than one-fourth thereafter. But in *USA Today* the proportion of American Muslim and Arab sources before 9/11 was greater than in the other three newspapers and remained quite high in the post-9/11 period.

The big "losers" in terms of being selected as news sources were non-Muslim local politicians in New York City, who constituted 16 percent of all sources in stories related to American Muslims and Arabs in the year before 9/11, but plunged to a tiny share of 1 percent in the six months thereafter. This steep decline occurred in all three New York newspapers. National public officials and politicians, who accounted for 13 percent of the sources before 9/11, were less affected and held on to a 10 percent share of the four newspapers' total pool of sources in the months after 9/11. While the news media's tendency to rely on authoritative sources in politics and other walks of public life was reflected in the news about Muslim Americans before the terrorist attacks, it nearly disappeared after 9/11 with respect to local politicians and weakened concerning national public officials.

FROM PARTISAN CONTROVERSIES TO
CIVIL LIBERTIES AND CIVIL RIGHTS ISSUES

Before September 11, 2001, the predominant news themes that related to American Muslims and American Arabs were taken from local, domestic, and international politics. Typically, this sort of news focused on partisan controversies, especially during election campaigns, and concerned one or the other candidate's relationships with American Muslim and/or Arab individuals or groups with alleged sympathies for or ties to terrorists and terrorist organizations in the Middle East. This became a prominent issue in the fall of 2000, when published reports revealed that the Republican presidential candidate, George W. Bush, had received $1,000 and the Democratic candidate in the New York race for the U.S. Senate, Hillary Clinton, $50,000 for their respective campaigns from American Muslim groups. Because of New York City's large bloc of Jewish voters, these revelations became hot issues in the city. In the last stage of the race, the *Daily News* reported that the First Lady's campaign had benefited from a fundraiser thrown by an American Muslim organization and thereby provided Clinton's opponent Rick Lazio and the New York State Republican Party with ammunition to attack her as proterrorist and anti-Israel. While literally all news organizations in New York City (as well as the media elsewhere) reported on what became the central campaign issue, the *New York Post* was especially relentless in bashing Mrs. Clinton for her alleged ties to alleged terrorist-friendly organizations and individuals. The following lines were quite typical for the *Post's* tirades:

> Do you believe that Israel has a right to exist?
> Do you believe that America needs a dependable, democratic ally in the strategically vital, oil-rich Middle East?
> Then Hillary's record should really give you pause.
>
> * Before becoming First Lady, Hillary chaired the New World Foundation—an organization that funded groups controlled by the Palestinian Liberation Organization. And this was back when even liberals considered the PLO a terrorist group.
> * Over the years, she's befriended Arab- and Muslim-American organizations that refuse to denounce—and often defend—terrorist groups. . . .
> * And just last month, frequent White House guest Nihad Awad, of the Council on American-Islamic Relations, railed against the notion of Arab coexistence with Israel, preaching instead the virtues of violence—and of Arab plans to reclaim "all Palestine."
>
> Hillary's response?
> None to speak of.[36]

While American Muslims were mentioned by journalists, commentators, and all kinds of non-Muslim sources in the news about what the *Daily News* called Mrs. Clinton's "Mideast problem," they did not get a great deal of access to the media to speak to the issue themselves. An article in the *Daily News* was among the exceptions in that it quoted Dr. Ahmad Jaber, an American Muslim and New York City resident, who had voted for Democrats in the past but said he would vote for Republicans this time around.

According to the newspaper, "New York Muslims yesterday seemed more upset with Hillary Clinton over the donation issue [and for returning the donations] even though it was Clinton's GOP opponent, Rick Lazio, who called the funds "blood money."[37] According to this article, Muslim Americans were less upset about the fact that presidential candidate George W. Bush sent back $1,000 to an American Muslim organization. But, as the *New York Times* put it, Clinton and Lazio "battled intensely . . . over each other's loyalty to Israel, signaling the extraordinary emphasis on Jewish voters in the final days of their race."[38]

A year later, the issue of American Muslims and their connections to terrorist groups abroad made the headlines once again, when it entered into the Democratic primary races in New York City. A coalition of American Muslim groups that had endorsed one of the mayoral candidates, Mark Green, and three candidates for borough presidencies, withdrew its endorsements after a state assemblyman had gone public with the accusation that members of the coalition had links to terrorist groups in the Middle East. In the midst of the ensuing controversy, the coalition withdrew its endorsements, hoping not to damage the chances of the candidates of its choice. In a departure from the news that dwelled on this immediate campaign issue, *New York Times* reporter Jennifer Steinhauer addressed the broader problem of American Muslims trying to participate in the city's political process when she wrote, "The inability for any candidate to do business with Muslim groups without taking heat raises questions about whether Muslims, who have gained some political power in places like Detroit, will ever be able to get a foothold in New York."[39] The dominance of news about Muslim and Arab Americans' involvement in the American body politic and the frequently mentioned allegations that these minorities had ties to or sympathized with terrorists in the Middle East diminished in the months after 9/11. There was also less news about the American Muslims' religious observances, holidays, or customs. Instead, the news media paid a great deal of attention to the government's curbs on civil liberties and civil rights as they affected Muslims and Arabs in the United States. Before the attacks on the World Trade Center and the Pentagon, these topics were not particularly prominent, comprising only 6 percent of the total themes in the four newspapers' combined coverage. After 9/11 there was a drastic change in this respect in that the four newspapers combined devoted about one-third of their total coverage of Muslims and Arabs in the United States on civil rights/civil liberties issues and the violation of those rights—including physical attacks on members of these groups.

Not surprisingly, 9/11 often took center stage in stories about American Muslims and Arabs, but perhaps surprisingly, it did so in mostly positive ways. For example, a wave of reports highlighted the patriotism of American Muslims and Arabs and downplayed the stereotype that members of these groups support terrorism. Headlines such as "Muslims in B'klyn call for peace" (*NY*

Post, September 17, 2001); "City Arabs & Muslims back U.S." (*NY Daily News,* October 8, 2001); "Public Lives: A daughter of Islam, and an enemy of terror" (*NY Times,* October 25, 2001) were quite common in the weeks and months after 9/11. In all, 9 percent of all discernible themes in this sort of news dealt directly with the terror of 9/11 as it affected the Muslim or Arab minorities.

There was also a surge in topics that dealt with the difficult life circumstances and identity problems of some American Muslims. The *New York Times,* for example, devoted several articles to this topic and, in some cases, managed to educate non-Muslim Americans about their Muslim fellow citizens. Thus, a twenty-one-year-old woman in Bridgeview, Illinois, told the *Times,* "I love Islam and I love anything in this country." But because her apparel identified her as a Muslim, "she also admitted that she is sad and fearful in the wake of 9/11."[40] But these stories also intensified the uneasy feelings in some non-Muslim Americans. Reporting on high school students in a private Islamic academy in Brooklyn, Susan Sachs wrote: "They are Americans who feel duty-bound by Islam to obey American laws. But some of them say that if their country called them to war against a Muslim army, they might refuse to fight. . . . Some of the students, for example, said they would support any leader who they decided was fighting for Islam."[41] Another story in the *Times* contained a quote by a female college student who said: "In high school I was asking myself, am I more Pakistani or more American. Being Muslim answers that question." Her friend was even more specific when she said: "I am Muslim first, not even American Muslim. Because so much of the American culture is directly in conflict with my values as a Muslim, I can't identify solely as an American, or even as an American Muslim."[42] The question of whether the views of some of these teenagers were representative among young American Muslims was not discussed in these kinds of articles that typically reflected an understanding for the plight of American Muslims but raised troubling questions in the minds of some, perhaps many, readers. Thus, the *Times* published a letter-to-the-editor that described one of these stories as "one of the more frightening you have published in memory" and continued, "Though raised in our free society, some might not fight for America against fellow Muslims. Imagine what we would think of Christian students who refused to fight Germany in World War II because Germans were Christians." The letter closed with this sentence: "If the views of these young Muslim Americans are at all typical, we are in trouble."[43]

SUPPORT FOR THE CIVIL LIBERTIES OF
AMERICAN MUSLIMS AND ARABS

We mentioned above that civil liberties and civil rights of American Muslims and Arabs were the predominant topics in the months after 9/11. But the fact that a theme is more frequently covered than other topics does not tell us what views and opinions are expressed in the mass-mediated debate, whether in straight news articles, letters-to-the-editor, editorials, or op-ed articles. The following excerpts illustrate the range of viewpoints in the news media on the civil liberties/civil rights theme:

One day after 9/11 the *New York Times* published a letter-to-the-editor in which the reader pleaded:

> The inevitable temptation to change fundamentally the nature of our society, by attacking the civil rights and civil liberties of any individual or group, must be resisted.[44]

Addressing the controversy over racial and ethnic profiling of people "with Middle Eastern looks," columnist Stanley Crouch wrote in the *Daily News*:

> We have had war declared on us by a spider at the center of a web of terrorist cells. Followers of that spider are hiding in the Arab-American community. No one doubts this. No one. In fact, it should bother all of us that a moratorium was not declared on immigration from the Middle East after the 1993 attack on the twin towers, especially since most of those identified with Sept. 11 arrived here after that time. . . .
>
> If more Americans are murdered by people who are part of the terrorist web from the Middle East and successfully hiding out in a certain community, the response is going to have less to do with any kind of bigotry than with the icy nature of war.[45]

And while attacks on Arabs and Muslims were increasingly reported in the news, one commentator praised in the *New York Post* "the breathtaking paucity of violence against Muslims and Arabs."[46] This was a stunning assessment at a time when President George W. Bush, during a visit to the Islamic Center in Washington, DC, denounced violence against Muslim and Arab Americans, saying,

> Those who feel like they can intimidate our fellow citizens to take out their anger don't represent the best of America, they represent the worst of humankind, and they should be ashamed of that kind of behavior.[47]

After 9/11, voices that defended the civil liberties and civil rights of American Muslims and Arabs were more numerous in the mass-mediated debate than were those who advocated curbing those freedoms: Of all positions mentioned in the news about Muslim and Arab citizens and residents, 15 percent expressed their support for unfettered civil liberties and civil rights for these minorities, while 5 percent were against protecting these fundamental freedoms for Muslim and Arab Americans. Before 9/11, these issues were not frequently discussed in the news media, counting for only 2 percent of all pertinent positions—1 percent each for and against protecting these rights for the Muslim and Arab minorities. While differing in degree, the post-9/11 debate on civil liberties and civil rights of American Muslims and Arabs was in all four newspapers substantially tilted in favor of those who supported American Muslims' and Arabs' fundamental freedoms.

When the issue of American Muslims' and Arabs' alleged support of terrorism came up in the news before 9/11, twice as many voices made this allegation expressly or implicitly than rejected this proposition. But after 9/11, there was a complete turnaround in the newspapers mentioned: twice as many voices opposed the notion that Muslim and Arab Americans support terrorists than made this accusation.

Before 9/11, when positions on Israel were expressed in stories that also mentioned or were exclusively about Muslim or Arab Americans, more revealed anti-Israel rather than pro-Israel views. There were far fewer references to the Jewish state in pertinent post-9/11 articles, but when this issue was addressed by sources, the reported viewpoints were equally divided between anti- and pro-Israel sentiments.

MORE POSITIVE DESCRIPTIONS OF
MUSLIM AMERICANS AFTER 9/11

Surprisingly, the textual depiction of American Muslims and Arabs in the news was more positive and less negative in the wake of the terrorist events of 9/11 than before the event. Whereas one-fourth of the pertinent articles in the four newspapers were categorized by our coders as positive or supportive before 9/11, better than four in ten described these minorities in a sympathetic light after the attacks. Similarly, the stories that painted American Muslims and Arabs in a negative light decreased from nearly one-third before 9/11 to less than one-fourth afterwards (see table 1.3). In the *Times* and *Post* the share of positive stories grew significantly after 9/11, in the *Daily News* only modestly. And while negative depictions of American Muslims and Arabs decreased after "Black Tuesday" in the *Times* and *Post*, the share of negative stories went up in the *Daily News* and *USA Today*. These differences are best explained by the negligible percentage of negative stories and the high share of positive articles in *USA Today* before the terror strikes. In the *Daily News*, too, the proportion of stories that our coders perceived as negative was significantly lower before 9/11 than in the *Times* and *Post*. Regardless of these differences, three of the newspapers (*Times, Post,* and *USA Today*) depicted American Muslims and Arabs more favorably than unfavorably after 9/11, and the fourth newspaper (*Daily News*) carried an equal share of positive and negative articles.

Table 1.3 Depiction of American Muslims and Arabs before and after 9/11 in Four Daily Newspapers (*New York Times, New York Daily News, New York Post,* and *USA Today*)

	12 Months before 9/11	6 Months after 9/11	Change
	(%)	(%)	(%)
Positive	9	17	+ 8
Probl. Positive	16	25	+ 9
Neutral/Ambiguous	44	36	− 8
Probl. Negative	21	14	− 7
Negative	10	8	− 2
	N=210	N=643	

N = Number of stories
Source: Muslims in New York City Project

THE RISE OF THEMATIC NEWS

As mentioned above, television news in particular is overwhelmingly episodic and narrowly focused on specific events, issues, or developments at the expense of thematic approaches that report more extensively on the larger context (Iyengar 1991).[48] In the age of sound bites, there is less opportunity for thematic reporting. Increasingly, newspapers opt for short, snappy news and episodic frames at the expense of in-depth reporting. Following the terrorist attacks of September 11, the news about American Muslims and Arabs in the four newspapers combined changed from overwhelmingly episodic to mostly thematic. The ratio in the twelve months before 9/11 was 60 percent to 30 percent in favor of episodic stories, with the rest fairly equally divided between episodic and thematic reporting modes. In contrast, after the terrorist attacks on U.S. soil about half of all relevant stories were framed overwhelmingly as thematic and four of ten mostly as episodic. While these changes were most pronounced in the reporting of the *Times* and *Daily News,* the *Post,* too, decreased the ratio of episodic stories and increased the share of thematically framed articles. *USA Today* marched to its own drummer, switching from more thematically framed stories before 9/11 to slightly more episodic articles thereafter.[49] Because *USA Today* comes closest to a printed version of television news, we did not expect to find more stories with thematic than episodic frames in either of the time periods we studied. Perhaps the best explanation is that the more thematic framing mode in the pre-9/11 months was an aberration, the result of a very small number of stories about Muslim Americans that typically described interesting aspects of this minority and were best told in thematic or contextual frames. After the attacks of 9/11, American

Muslims and Arabs were far more frequently covered and mentioned in this newspaper—often in short and typically episodically framed news items or paragraphs. But again, except for *USA Today*, thematic framing increased and episodic framing decreased in the newspapers we examined.

FEW DIFFERENCES IN LOCAL AND NATIONAL COVERAGE

The similarities in the coverage of Muslims and Arabs in the New York metropolitan area on the one hand and in the national setting on the other were far more striking than the differences. Thus, in both geographical settings local and national politicians were the dominant sources before 9/11, followed by Muslim Americans and media-based sources. But in New York City, with a much larger percentage of Muslim population than in the nation as a whole, Muslim Americans' share of the total sources in the local news media was larger before and after 9/11 than in the national coverage. Not surprisingly, local politicians were cited more often in the New York metropolitan context, members of the Bush administration and Congress more often in the national news coverage.

Local, state, national, and international politics and policies that referred to American Muslims in one way or the other were by far the most covered topics in both the New York City and the nationwide context before September 11, 2001, while civil liberties/civil rights issues affecting the Muslim and Arab minorities were the most often-covered themes in the months after 9/11 in both New York metropolitan and national news. The only difference with respect to positions and opinions expressed by sources was one of degree. Before 9/11 pro-Israel and anti-Israel voices were more frequently mentioned in the local New York City news, whereas support for protecting the civil liberties of American Muslims and Arabs was more often expressed in national reporting than in New York metropolitan area news.

In both local and national news there was a shift from overwhelmingly episodic coverage before 9/11 to a mostly thematic framing pattern after 9/11. It is noteworthy, however, that this change was more pronounced in the local news than the national news, probably because of the substantial Muslim population in New York City and surrounding areas.

Finally, the earlier-described partisan infighting about American Muslims' support for various election campaigns in New York City and New York state explains why the portrayal of Muslim and Arab Americans was perceived by our coders as more negative in the pertinent local news than in the national coverage. But after 9/11, these differences diminished, with positive stories outscoring negative articles in both the local and national context.

MUSLIM AND ARAB AMERICANS IN TELEVISION NEWS

In the twelve months before 9/11 CBS-TV's *Early Show* and the *Evening News with Dan Rather* aired only seven stories mentioning Muslim and/or Arab Americans, compared to fifty-one such stories in the six months after the terror in New York and Washington, DC. Thus, a comparison between the pre-9/11 and post-9/11 coverage seems to be not very meaningful. Yet, our analysis demonstrated that television news changed mostly in the same directions as newspaper reporting did. One of the exceptions was the dominance of journalistic sources before and after 9/11 that was far more pronounced than in the print press—a tendency observed with respect to television coverage in general.[50] But the share of media-based sources shrank in CBS's news from more than half of all sources before 9/11 to more than one-third after 9/11. In the sparse CBS News coverage of Muslim Americans before 9/11, about 10 percent of all interviewees or sources were identified as local or national politicians, while no Muslim American was interviewed or mentioned as a source at all. After 9/11, however, nearly one-fourth of all interviewees and sources in pertinent stories were members of these minorities, while the share of politicians remained constant. While American Muslims' religious customs and holidays were the topics of the pre-9/11 coverage, afterward CBS News, just like the print press, reported extensively on civil liberties issues as they affected Muslims and Arabs in the United States. Indeed, nearly two of five pertinent stories were devoted to this particular topic. However, contrary to the newspaper coverage, which was strongly tilted in favor of voices that rejected curbs on Muslim and Arab Americans' civil liberties and rights, television coverage showed a less pronounced advantage in favor of these positions.

Television news tends to be significantly more episodic than reporting in the print media. Yet, just as we found in the reporting of newspapers, there was a decline of episodic stories in CBS newscasts after 9/11 and an increase in thematic segments, so that about the same number of overwhelmingly episodic and thematic stories were aired.

DISCUSSION OF FINDINGS

The terrorist attacks of 9/11 changed the ways in which newspapers and television news reported about Muslim and Arab Americans. We found that there was a distinct shift from a limited and stereotypical coverage in the pre-9/11 period to a more comprehensive, inclusive, and less stereotypical news presentation thereafter. Besides covering and referring to Muslim and Arab Americans more frequently and featuring pertinent stories more prominently in the post-9/11 period, reporters and editors selected American

Muslims and Arabs far more frequently as interviewees and sources after the catastrophic attacks on New York and Washington than in the months before. Or, to put it differently, the preferential news treatment of officialdom and authoritative sources weakened as a result of the 9/11 disaster in stories that reported on the Muslim and Arab minorities. Moreover, in the wake of the terrorist nightmare, the print media were more inclined to publish news analyses, columns, and letters-to-the-editor concerning Muslim and Arab Americans and thereby contributed to or even initiated mass-mediated debates concerning these minorities in their pages.

Probably the most important change occurred in the choice of news topics and how they were reported. Before 9/11 by far the most prominent news theme concerned Muslim and Arab Americans who participated in the political process, or tried to do so, especially during election campaigns, but were accused of sympathizing with or supporting terrorists in the Middle East. We are not suggesting that the press should have ignored these political controversies, but we do note that the news media failed to cover other aspects of American Muslim life as frequently and extensively. As it was, the two-dimensional perspective that Montague Kern traced in foreign news reporting was strongly reflected in the pre-9/11 coverage of Muslim and Arab Americans in that foreign or international issues and events colored the domestic story in stereotypical ways.[51] While this did not disappear completely in the post-9/11 period, the more frequent use of Muslim and Arab Americans as sources resulted in a more balanced presentation of the news.

After 9/11, the predominant themes, especially the status of the civil liberties and civil rights of American Muslims and Arabs, arose from the reactions to an unprecedented terrorist attack that was perpetrated by Arabs and Muslims. But in spite of the context in which these issues arose, there was no jump in stereotypical coverage. Perhaps that was the consequence of news items reporting on public figures' pleas for a better understanding between Muslims and non-Muslims in the United States, and their assurances that most Muslims here and abroad have absolutely nothing to do with terrorism and that the religion of Islam does not preach violence. Just as important, there was significantly more support in the mass-mediated discourse for protecting the civil liberties and rights of American Muslims and Arabs than for curbing their freedoms. Large parts of the post-9/11 news topics that concerned or touched on the interests of Muslim and Arab Americans were framed by domestic rather than foreign story lines.

Another positive change was the increase in thematic and the decrease of episodic news frames in the months after September 11. When stories provide readers with more than bare-boned facts and explain news events in a larger context, news consumers get more comprehensive information and are able to make their evaluation of individuals and groups on a more informed and educated basis. Taken together, these changes added up to a significantly more positive and less negative media coverage of American Muslims and Arabs.

Since most Americans' knowledge about Muslim Americans is to a large extent based on media reports, not personal encounters, we wondered whether the changes in the pertinent news content affected the ways in which the American public viewed the Muslim minority in the months after September 11, 2001. Opinion surveys revealed that two months after the attacks on New York and Washington the American public viewed Muslim Americans significantly more favorably than before. Moreover, after a huge increase in the volume of coverage after 9/11, fewer survey respondents said that they had never heard of Muslim Americans or that they could not rate their attitude towards them. While they were still more favorably inclined toward the Muslim minority than before 9/11, this spike in positive attitudes already showed signs of decline by February 2002. (For a far more comprehensive account of the American public's attitudes towards Muslim Americans and Muslim and Islam in general see chapter 4.)

When Americans are faced with grave national crises, racial and ethnic prejudices tend to sweep away support for the constitutionally guaranteed civil liberties of whole groups whose loyalties are questioned. This was especially true for Japanese Americans in World War II. As one observer concluded more than twenty years before 9/11,

> The racism that led to the internment of Japanese-Americans during World War II was created partly by the motion picture industry, which for years typecast Orientals as villains, and partly by the press, especially the newspapers of William Randolph Hearst. . . . The "yellow peril" hysteria and the stereotyping which helped produce that myth have retreated into history. The Arab has now become the latest victim of media stereotyping.[52]

After 9/11 and following the news of physical and verbal attacks on Muslim Americans and on people wrongly thought to be Muslims, a number of media organizations reported how Japanese Americans recalled the persecution during World War II. The explicit or implicit message here was that it would be wrong to repeat the mistakes of the past. In the six months after 9/11, U.S. newspapers and wire services that were available in the Lexis-Nexis archive published a total of 109 such stories; ABC News, CBS News, NBC News, CNN, and National Public Radio combined aired nine segments that recalled the treatment of Japanese Americans in the context of Muslim and Arab Americans' post-9/11 predicament. One day after 9/11, for example, John Donvan said in his report on ABC-TV's *World News Tonight*,

> Any common American will tell you immigrants from Middle-Eastern countries are as law abiding as anyone. They have unusually strong family values.

They mostly vote Republican. But Oklahoma City happened in 1995 and they all felt like suspects. Now the World Trade Center, and they feel like it's happening again. The principle at work here is guilt by association.[53]

And the *Seattle Post-Intelligencer*'s Joshua Sanders mentioned in a story about the painful memories of Japanese Americans,

Like Arab Americans and Muslims who have been the targets of anger and violence during the last week, Japanese Americans—particularly those who survived the internment camps of World War II—remember the same treatment. They, too, were targeted and punished because of their heritage.[54]

The media reported also that leaders like President Bush and New York's mayor Rudy Giuliani urged Americans not to direct their anger towards ethnic and religious minorities. These kinds of appeals probably had some effects on public opinion.

To sum up, then, the events of 9/11 forced the media to cover the Muslim and Arab minorities more frequently. In a strange way, this caused the press to present news consumers with a more comprehensive picture of these groups. One result was that the news media granted Muslim Americans in particular more access after 9/11 and that members of this minority made themselves available to the media. The limited news about Muslim and Arab Americans, the prevalent topics, and the more episodic than thematic framing patterns before 9/11 added up to more negative and stereotypical associations than the more frequent reporting, the different topics, and the dominance of thematic frames in the post-9/11 months. As one expert in the field has pointed out, the cultures and peoples of the Middle East "are not easily explained in quick two-minute network news stories."[55] The same holds true for episodically framed stories in the print media.

After we completed the research described in this chapter, we wondered whether the positive post-9/11 changes were a temporary phenomenon or signaled a more durable shift in the way the U.S. news media reports on Muslim and Arab citizens and residents. We answer this question in the next chapter, which is based on additional research in the weeks before and after the first 9/11 anniversary and the years thereafter.

NOTES

1. See, for example, Jack Shaheen, *Arab and Muslim Stereotypes in American Popular Culture* (Washington, DC: Center for Muslim-Christian Understanding, 1997), and *Reel Bad Arabs: How Hollywood Vilifies a People* (Northampton, MA: Interlink Publishing Group, 2001); and Reeva Simon, *The Middle East in Crime Fiction* (New York: Lilian Barber Press, 1989).

2. The reviewer was Adil Sohail Qureshi, and the comment concerned Jack Shaheen's book *Reel Bad Arabs: How Hollywood Vilifies a People*. See *www.amazon.com/exdec/obidos/ASIN/1566563887/ref=pd_sim.../002-929853-184886* (accessed October 22, 2001).

3. Simon, *Middle East in Crime Fiction*, 140.

4. Edward W. Said, *Covering Islam: How the Media and the Experts Determine how we see the Rest of the World* (New York: Pantheon Books, 1981), 26.

5. The focus groups were conducted for the Muslims in New York City project by researchers at Columbia University.

6. For more on the sentiments of Muslim high school students at the Al Noor School see Susan Sachs, "The 2 Worlds of Muslim-American Teenagers," *New York Times*, October 9, 2001.

7. The quote is from Ben McGrath, "Brooklyn Boycott," *New Yorker*, July 22, 2002, 24. Although it was not clear whether and to what extent the initiative was successful and affected the *Post's* circulation, people at the newspaper were concerned enough to dispatch marketing and promotion people to meet with boycott leaders.

8. The first ever systematic poll of American Muslims was conducted for Project MAPS: Muslims in American Public Square by Zogby International. See *www.projectmap.com/PMReport.htm*.

9. Walter Lippmann, *Public Opinion* (1922; repr. New York: Free Press, 1997).

10. Russel W. Neumann, Marion Just, and Ann N. Crigler, *Common Knowledge* (Chicago: University of Chicago Press, 1992), 11.

11. Pippa Norris, *Women, Media, and Politics* (New York: Oxford University Press), 2.

12. Robert M. Entman, "Reporting Environmental Policy Debate: The Real Media Bias," *Harvard International Journal of Press/Politics* 1, no. 3 (1996): 77, 78.

13. W. Lance Bennett, "An Introduction to Journalism Norms and Representations of Politics," *Political Communication* 13, no. 4 (1996): 377.

14. Montague Kern, "The Invasion of Afghanistan: Domestic vs. Foreign Stories," in *Television Coverage of the Middle East*, ed. William C. Adams (Norwood, NJ: Ablex Publishing, 1981), 106.

15. Shanto Iyengar, *Is Anyone Responsible?* (Chicago: University of Chicago Press, 1991), 26–45.

16. For more on these stereotypes see Christopher P. Campbell, *Race, Myth, and the News* (Thousand Oaks, CA: Sage, 1995); Robert M. Entman and Andrew Rojecki, *The Black Image in the White Mind* (Chicago: University of Chicago Press, 2000); and Brigitte L. Nacos and Nastasha Hritzuk, "The Portrayal of Black America in the Mass Media," in *Black and Multicultural Politics in America*, ed. M. Alex Assensoh and Lawrence Hanks (New York: New York University Press, 2000), 165–95.

17. Entman and Rojecki, *Black Image in the White Mind*, 207.

18. For more interesting aspects of news reporting on minorities see Bradley S. Greenberg, "Minorities and the Mass Media," in *Perspectives on Media Effects*, Jennings Bryant and Dolf Zillmann eds. (Hillsdale, NJ: Lawrence Erlbaum, 1986), 165–88.

19. Advisory Board's Report to the President, *One America in the 21st Century: Forging a New Future*, prepublication copy issued by the White House, September 18, 1998, 97.

20. Todd Gitlin, *The Whole World is Watching* (Berkeley, CA: University of California Press, 1980), 7.

21. Herbert Gans, *Deciding What's News* (New York: Vintage Books, 1979), 61.

22. David K. Shipler, "Blacks in the Newsrooms. Progress? Yes, but . . .," *Columbia Journalism Review* (May/June 1998), 28.

23. Sig Gissler, "Newspapers Quest for Racial Candor," *Media Studies Journal* 8, no. 3 (1994): 123.

24. Martin Gilens, *Why Americans Hate Welfare: Race, Media, and the Politics of Antipoverty Policy* (Chicago: University of Chicago Press, 1999), 150–53.

25. We do not know how many Muslim and Arab Americans work in the nonethnic press in the United States because professional journalism organizations keep track only of the numbers of Black, Hispanic, and Asian Americans in the news media; but we suspect that the numbers of Muslim and Arab Americans in the newsrooms are rather small.

26. Although it is part of the Muslims in New York City project, this study examines the news about Muslim Americans both in New York and across the United States, assuming that the perceptions of Muslim and non-Muslim New Yorkers are affected not only by local news but by national reporting as well. Indeed, for some of the following chapters we also include an analysis of photographs in the print media and TV visuals of Muslims abroad because we are convinced that such images (as well as the spoken and written words about non-American Muslims) also affect what Muslim and non-Muslim Americans think about each other and about news reporting biases in this context.

27. See, for example, Dr. Barry A. Kosmin and Dr. Egon Mayer, "Profile of the U.S. Muslim Population," ARIS Report No. 2, October 2001, The Graduate Center of the City University of New York.

28. Interview with Louis Abdellatif Cristillo, Columbia University, July 25, 2002.

29. The research was part of the ongoing Muslims in New York City project at Columbia University. The canvassing was conducted between 1998 and 1999.

30. For the coverage of anti-American terrorism in the 1980s and the early 1990s, see Brigitte L. Nacos, *Terrorism and the Media: From the Iran Hostage Crisis to the World Trade Center Bombing* (New York: Columbia University Press, 1996).

31. For the uniformity of TV news broadcasts see David L. Altheide, "Three-in-one News: Network Coverage of Iran," *Journalism Quarterly* 59 (1982): 482–86.

32. Stephen Kaufman, "American Museum of Natural History stages events about Islam," *usinfo.state.gov/usa/islam/a013002a.htm*.

33. "A spiritual Awakening: Religion in the Media, Dec. 2000–Nov. 2001," study prepared by Douglas Gould & Co. for the Ford Foundation.

34. For the publicity imperative of terrorists see Brigitte L. Nacos, *Mass-Mediated Terrorism: The Central Role of the Media in Terrorism and Counterterrorism* (Lanham, MD: Rowman & Littlefield, 2002).

35. For the preponderance of journalistic sources in TV news see Matthew Robert Kerbel, *Edited for Television* (Boulder, CO: Westview Press, 1994); for the prominence of journalistic sources in the print press see Brigitte L. Nacos, *The Press, Presidents, and Crises* (New York: Columbia University Press, 1990).

36. "Hillary's World," *New York Post*, October 26, 2000, 44.

37. Leslie Casimir, "Anger among N.Y. Muslims: React to Hillary Return of money," *New York Daily News*, October 30, 2000, 6.

38. Randal C. Archibold and Adam Nagourney, "Lazio and Clinton swap charges," *New York Times*, November 4, 2000, 1.

39. Jennifer Steinhauer, "Political Memo: On the road to endorsements by ethnic groups, mayoral hopefuls fall into potholes," *New York Times*, August 10, 2001, B3.

40. John W. Fountain, "Sadness and fear as they feel doubly vulnerable," *New York Times*, October 5, 2001, 10.

41. Susan Sachs, "The 2 Worlds of Muslim-American teenagers," *New York Times*, Oct. 7, 2001.

42. Laurie Goldstein, "A nation challenged: Islamic Traditions; Muslims nurture sense of self on campus," *New York Times*, November 3, 2001, B1.

43. "America at War: Voices in a nation on edge. Roles of religion," *New York Times*, October 9, 2001, A24.

44. The letter was written by John S. Koppel on September 11, 2001, and published in the *New York Times*, September 12, 2001, A26.

45. Stanley Crouch, "Drawing the line on racial profiling," *Daily News*, October 4, 2001, 41.

46. John Podhoretz, "Our fellow Americans—the friends within," *New York Post*, September 17, 2001, 41.

47. The President was quoted in Tamar Lewin and Gustav Niebuhr, "A Nation Challenged: Violence, Attacks and Harassment Continue on Middle Eastern people and mosques," *New York Times*, September 18, 2001, B5.

48. See Shanto Iyengar, *Is Anyone Responsible?* (Chicago: University of Chicago Press, 1991).

49. The ratio in the *Times* was 60 percent to 33 percent in favor of episodic stories before 9/11 and 51 percent to 33 percent in favor of thematic articles thereafter, with the rest of the stories being equally thematic and episodic. In the *Post* the pre-9/11 ratio was 57 percent to 32 percent in favor of episodically framed stories, 52 percent to 42 percent in favor of episodically framed articles afterwards. In the *Daily News*, 67 percent of the stories were episodic and 28 percent thematic before 9/11, 51 percent thematic and 41 percent episodic in the post–9/11 period. In sharp contrast, *USA Today* changed from a more thematic coverage (50 percent of the pertinent stories were mostly thematic and 36 percent episodic) before 9/11 to more episodic framing (48 percent episodic, 44 percent thematic) after the terror attacks.

50. During the 2000 presidential election campaign, for example, reporters received 74 percent of the pertinent airtime on the three broadcast networks ABC, CBS, and NBC, while the candidates themselves were granted 12 percent only, according to the Center for Media and Public Policy. See "Campaign 2000 Final," *Media Monitor* XIV, no. 6 (November/December 2000): 1–5.

51. Montague Kern, "The Invasion of Afghanistan: Domestic v. Foreign Stories," in *Television Coverage of the Middle East*, ed. William C. Adams, 106–27 (Norwood, NJ: Ablex Publishing, 1981).

52. Shaheen, *Reel Bad Arabs*, 89.

53. Donovan's report was aired on ABC's *World News Tonight* on September 12, 2001.

54. Joshua Sanders, "Japanese Americans see similarities to WWII conditions," *Seattle Post-Intelligencer*, September 18, 2001, A7.

55. Shaheen, *Arab and Muslim Stereotypes*, 104.

2

The First 9/11 Anniversary and Beyond

The first anniversary of the events of 9/11 offered an opportunity to test whether the more frequent, inclusive, contextual, and positive coverage of Muslims and Arabs in the New York area and across the country that we found for the immediate post-9/11 period survived beyond the acute crisis months. We found first of all that the positive trend continued with respect to the far greater frequency of news items devoted to Muslim and Arab Americans in both print and TV news. Moreover, while the share of sources identified as American Muslims and Arabs was not as pronounced as during the six months after 9/11, it remained higher than in the pre-9/11 period in the local and national print and broadcast news.

As far as the selection of news sources was concerned, the most notable change was caused by the continuing and indeed increased difficulties that Muslims and Arabs in New York and elsewhere in the United States encountered in the post-9/11 climate. Whereas 6 percent of all news sources were identified as police or other officials in the law enforcement and justice system in the six months after 9/11, these types of sources accounted for 12 percent of the total source pool during the first anniversary period. Again, this trend was very similar in the print media and in national and local television newscasts. Yet, while curbs on civil liberties affected members of the Muslim and Arab minority on the domestic front of the intensifying war on terrorism, these media organizations paid far less attention to civil liberties issues as they related to the plight of American Muslims and Arabs than they did in the six months immediately after 9/11. When these issues were covered, news sources tended to be more critical and less supportive of these minorities than in the weeks and months after the terrorist attacks. These changes were particularly striking in two respects: In the six months

after 9/11, only 4 percent of the expressed positions boiled down to the accusation that Muslims and Arabs in the United States are supportive of terrorists and terrorism, but around the first 9/11 anniversary 14 percent of all
discernible positions expressed this belief—a significant increase. Similarly,
during the anniversary period, only 4 percent of the cited views indicated
support for the civil liberties of the Muslim and Arab minorities, which was
a drastic decline from the 15 percent that supported them in the six months
after 9/11. On the *CBS Evening News with Dan Rather* more interviewees or
cited sources accused Muslim or Arab Americans of supporting terrorism
than denied this proposition. On the other hand, all of the few sources that
expressed an opinion on issues surrounding the civil liberties of Arabs and
Muslims supported the rights of these minorities. As for the two local television channels, they either did not report on these issues (Fox Channel
Five) or presented more sources that denied American Muslims' support for
terrorism than made such an accusation (WCBS).

SWITCH TO OVERWHELMINGLY NEGATIVE
PORTRAYALS OF AMERICAN MUSLIMS

In the immediate aftermath of 9/11, many opinion leaders, among them
President George W. Bush, urged Americans repeatedly not to blame the
Muslim and Arab communities in the United States collectively for the terrorist deeds of a few. But as time went by, most of these voices fell silent and
left the field to those who stirred sentiments that fueled prejudice and discrimination. By the time the first 9/11 anniversary came around the news
reflected this shift toward more critical and negative positions vis-à-vis
members of the Muslim and Arab communities. Given these changes, it was
not surprising that our coders categorized significantly more news stories in
the four newspapers as negative or critical of American Muslims and Arabs
than positive or supportive. This was a turnaround from the six months following the 9/11 attacks (see table 2.1).

On the *CBS Evening News with Dan Rather* the portrayal of Muslim and
Arab Americans changed from overwhelmingly positive in the post-9/11
months to very negative during the pre- and post-anniversary weeks. The
same trend was discernible in the local news of the Fox channel in the New
York area. The exception was the local evening TV news on WCBS in New
York, where the coverage was actually more positive with respect to Muslim
and Arab Americans than in the immediate post-9/11 months.

Although our project focused on stories about Muslims and Arabs in the
United States in general or on individual members of these groups, many
articles referred to Muslims and Arabs overseas as well. For this reason, we
wondered how Muslims and Arabs abroad were depicted in these articles

Table 2.1 Depiction of Muslim and Arab Americans in the Print Media

	6 months after 9/11	Before and after the first 9/11 anniversary	Change
	(%)	(%)	(%)
Positive/Supportive	17	9	-8
Probl. Positive	25	12	-13
Neutral/Ambiguous	36	37	+1
Probl. Negative	14	19	+5
Negative/Critical	8	24	+16
	N=643	N=127	

N = Number of stories
Source: Muslims in New York City Project

and broadcast segments. While their depiction was more negative than positive before and immediately after 9/11, we found a significant shift toward an even more one-sided depiction in the anniversary period.

One of the old and still valid journalistic tools of inquiry requires reporters to provide answers to the five Ws—who, what, when, where, and why. Thematic or contextual news demands reporting that transcends the limited scope of the first four Ws and pays particular attention to explaining the "why" of whatever triggers the news. For example, a news item simply conveying the information that a certain number of New Yorkers of Muslim and/or Arab descent are held in detention facilities based on tougher antiterrorism measures constitutes episodic reporting; thematic coverage would report on actual cases, the legal provisions guiding the incarceration of members of these groups, and similar background information. Unfortunately, the spike in thematic news at the expense of episodic reporting that we documented in the wake of 9/11 was not a durable switch as far as newspaper coverage was concerned. In the weeks before and after the first 9/11 anniversary close to two-thirds of the stories in the four newspapers we examined were overwhelmingly episodic (compared to 39 percent in the six months after 9/11) and only two of ten were mostly thematic (versus half of all stories in the immediate post-9/11 period). Television news was a mixed bag in terms of these framing patterns. In the *CBS Evening News with Dan Rather* relevant segments were evenly split between overwhelmingly episodic and thematic frames. In this respect, then, the network did not fall back into the dominant episodic framing patterns of the pre-9/11 period. Fox Channel Five's local news framed more stories in an episodic than a thematic mode, whereas the pertinent local news of WCBS was thoroughly episodic.

Summing up, then, we found evidence that the reporting patterns of the six months after 9/11 survived on two counts: Muslim and Arab Americans were more frequently covered and more often interviewed or cited as sources than before the events of September 11, 2001. But in all other respects the coverage retreated to the negative and stereotypical patterns of the pre-9/11 period—or worse. The news was less contextual, less balanced, and more negative and critical of Muslims and Arabs in the United States (and abroad) than in the immediate post-9/11 period. This coverage was not simply the result of different choices on the part of the news media but a reflection of the behavior of political leaders and other influential figures in the United States. In the wake of 9/11, prominent voices went public with the clear message that most Muslims and Arabs in America and elsewhere were as peaceful as most Christians, Jews, and adherents of other religions. But as the weeks and months passed, most of these influential voices went silent in this respect.

Several years after we conducted the first anniversary content analysis, we wondered how Muslim Americans fared in the media as more time went by. While we did not conduct a large-scale systematic content analysis, we relied on a qualitative examination of pertinent news items. The following section describes our observations.

BEYOND THE FIRST 9/11 ANNIVERSARY

The cartoon showed the entrance of a mosque, a "Call to Fatwah" sign with daily "Death to the Western Infidels" announcements, the distribution of "balloons & bombs for the kids," and a "Muslims for Peace and Understanding" group in which one member says, "Yes, this is somewhat unfortunate, but if it weren't for U.S. foreign policy . . ."[1] This was one cartoonist's reaction to a *fatwa* or religious edict against all terrorism that the members of the Fiqh Council of North America and Canada had issued three days earlier, on July 28, 2005. Indeed, on the day the fatwa was released, the same cartoonist depicted a suicide bomber with a "Quran" on a billboard that announced, "COMING SOON TO A THEATER, SHOPPING MALL & TRAIN STATION NEAR YOU . . ."[2]

In his reaction to the release of the fatwa, Washington, DC, radio talk show host Michael Graham described Islam as a "terrorist organization." Speaking of recent terrorism, Graham told listeners that the "problem is not extremism. The problem is Islam. We are at war with a terrorist organization named Islam."[3] According to the *Washington Post*, "Graham said 'Islam is a terrorist organization' 23 times" in this particular broadcast.[4] On

WNYC public radio's "Brian Lehrer Show," Steven Emerson attacked the fatwa as "bogus" and a public relation trick.[5]

As guest host of *The O'Reilly Factor* on the Fox News Network, John Kasich mentioned the antiterrorism pronouncement by "some American Muslim organizations" to introduce a videotaped conversation between Bill O'Reilly and evangelist Franklin Graham, who had denounced "Islam as a whole" as "evil" in the aftermath of the 9/11 attacks. While the audience received no information about the fatwa's content, they learned a great deal about Graham's view on an inherent chasm between Christians and Muslims. At one point, the Reverend Graham said, "But I want the American audience to understand the God that they [Muslims] worship is not the same God we worship. The God that I worship gave his son for me." Obviously speaking of the Christian-Islamic rift, he remarked, "I think we have to understand the religious aspect, and we're going to have to continue this war on terrorism. And it's not going to finish in Iraq. There are a number of other countries harboring terrorists right now, that support terrorists, that give to terrorists."[6]

In the months following 9/11, a plurality or majority of Americans believed that moderate Muslim leaders in the United States had not done enough to support the United States and denounce terrorism. The problem was that the news media did not report it prominently—or not at all—when Muslim leaders did speak out against the attacks of 9/11 or against terrorism in general. Indeed, the alleged silence of mainstream Muslim American leaders remained high on the agenda of conservative talk shows that perpetuated the myth of a uniformly silent leadership in the Muslim and Arab minorities—although several organizations publicized explicit condemnations of terrorism by leading Muslim individuals and groups on their web sites and in press releases. Still, up to the summer of 2005, North America's Muslim leaders did indeed fail to issue an official ruling or *fatwa* that categorically condemned all terrorist acts against civilians. Even those Muslims in North America who belonged to the attentive public were not of one mind on this issue. Several days after the antiterrorism *fatwa* was introduced, the following exchange occurred during a conversation between North American Muslims on PBS's *News Hour with Jim Lehrer* that dealt with the responsibility of Muslim leaders in America in a serious and comprehensive way:

> *Asra Nomani:* I think we know that the next [terrorist] attack can very much happen out of America. It's a matter of time; not whether it's going to happen, and our community in America will have failed if we don't confront the real problems that are being perpetrated in the name of our religion and basically betraying the faith. And our leadership needs to stand up for that.
>
> *Shadi Hamid:* I definitely agree with Asra. I think that our national Islamic organizations, even after 9/11, failed to effectively condemn terrorism and fight

extremism within our communities. For example, I mean, I think it is interesting how you've had all these suicide bombings almost daily in Iraq and Israel and of course we had 9/11. But how come this condemnation, why did we have to take three, four years for Muslim organizations to get together and issue a fatwa?

Imam Shaker Elsayed: I believe there is no apology for terrorism. We confronted it; we condemned it on 9/11, I personally signed a paper on behalf of the organization I worked for at that time and sent it everywhere to the press. I spoke with the press. So for Shadi to say, this is very late, this is—why did it take three years, it didn't take three years. It took you three years to note that there is something.[7]

Allie Shah addressed the same issue in an op-ed article in the Minneapolis *Star Tribune.* "Where are the moderate Muslims?" she asked at the outset. Her answer: "The better question might be: Why aren't you hearing us?" She, too, recognized a media-related public relations problem when she wrote, "The fact is that many prominent American Muslim groups have clearly and publicly denounced acts of terror in the name of Islam as barbaric, heinous and just plain wrong. Though they religiously send out press releases and e-mail statements after every attack, somehow their message doesn't seem to penetrate."[8]

Coming on the heels of the deadly attacks on the London transit system on July 7, 2005, and the release of an antiterrorist fatwa by Muslim scholars in the United Kingdom, the religious edict by Muslim leaders in North America was a first, and thus it was an important event. The text was unequivocal and contained the following rulings as its centerpiece:

1. All acts of terrorism targeting civilians are haram (forbidden) in Islam.
2. It is haram for a Muslim to cooperate with any individual or group that is involved in any act of terrorism or violence.
3. It is a civic and religious duty of Muslims to cooperate with law enforcement authorities to protect the lives of all civilians.[9]

Although this fatwa was released during a press conference at the National Press Club in Washington, DC, the news coverage in the mainstream media was spotty and not at all prominent. Both the *New York Times* and the *Washington Post* published stories of modest length (618 and 452 words respectively) about the forthcoming fatwa's content on pages 14 and 11 on the day the news conference was held.[10] There were no follow-up stories in the *Times* and *Post* the next day. While National Public Radio carried short news items on several programs and while the fatwa triggered the above-mentioned segment on PBS's *News Hour with Jim Lehrer* on the responsibilities of mainstream Muslims in America, most broadcast networks and many newspapers paid little or no attention to the initiative. The *Brian Lehrer Show* on WNYC public radio was probably the only non-Muslim media source that made the most important part of the fatwa's text available to its audience, when host Lehrer read its central paragraph. Altogether, the hundreds of newspapers that are archived by LexisNexis carried only forty-three news items on the release of the fatwa—many of them buried in short news summaries.[11]

All this demonstrated the no-win situation of American Muslim leaders in this particular respect: They were damned for not speaking out loudly and consistently against terrorism, and they were damned and doubted as to their sincerity when they did. But mostly they were ignored when they took stands against terrorism and terrorists.

As the number of religious hate crimes against Muslims and against persons mistakenly believed to be Muslims skyrocketed in the United Kingdom in the weeks after the attacks on London's transit system—in London alone there was a 600 percent increase in such crimes compared to the same period of the previous year—fear of anti-Muslim sentiments and actual attacks increased among Muslims in America as well. There was reason for such anxieties because harassment of and hate crimes against Muslims in the United States had remained high in the post-9/11 years. For 2004, one Muslim advocacy group documented more than 1,500 cases of harassment and anti-Muslim violence that included 141 cases of hate crimes, compared to about 1,000 such cases with 93 identified hate crimes a year earlier.[12] But these kinds of statistics, too, failed to get prominent news coverage.

We mentioned in chapter 1 that professional journalists, editors, and others in the news media recognize their responsibility to report not just on the majority population but on important aspects of all kinds of societal groups and thus also on Muslim and Arab Americans—their religion, their daily lives, their viewpoints, and their difficulties—at times when most anti-American and anti-Western terrorism is perpetrated by fanatics who misuse Islam for their purposes. The Society of Professional Journalists recognized this particular responsibility after 9/11, when the organization adopted "Guidelines for Countering Racial, Ethnic, and Religious Profiling" less than a month after 9/11.[13] Here are only a few of the guidelines for journalists that seem particularly relevant in the context of this chapter:

- Use language that is informative and not inflammatory;
- Portray Muslims, Arabs and Middle Easterners and South Asian Americans in the richness of their diverse experiences;
- Make an extra effort to include olive-complexioned and darker men and women, Sikhs, Muslims and devout religious people of all types in arts, business, society columns, and all other news and feature coverage, not just stories about the [terrorist] crisis.

Of course, one precondition for news media reflecting the richness and diversity of Muslim Americans is that communities and groups within a particular minority are covered regularly. In terms of the sheer volume of coverage, Muslim Americans fared far better in the media after 9/11 than they did before, as the research presented in this and the previous chapter establishes. This increased media attention continued well beyond the first 9/11 anniversary. Thus, in the year from July 1, 2004 to June 30, 2005, the newspapers and wire services archived by LexisNexis published 1,661 relevant news items compared to only 685 articles in the pre-9/11 period from July 1, 2000, to June 30, 2001.[14] To be sure, many of these stories reported about charges against individuals, groups, and organizations and their alleged support of anti-American terrorism. Equally prominent were reports on Muslims in America who fought for their right to wear head scarves or beards or observe their religion's precepts otherwise. But there were also stories that informed and educated readers on the richness and diversity in the American Muslim minority and thus followed the thoughtful recommendations of the Society of Professional Journalists. Some newspapers made far greater efforts in this respect than many others.

ONE NEWSPAPER'S EXEMPLARY REPORTING

Newsday, owned by the Tribune Company and mostly read by residents of Suffolk and Nassau Counties on Long Island and the adjacent New York City borough of Queens, provides exemplary coverage of minority groups in these areas, in all of New York City, and even in the national setting. The way this newspaper reported on the lives and activities of Muslim and Arab Americans was particularly impressive after 9/11 in terms of the frequency of coverage, the choice of topics, and the incorporation of Muslim voices and viewpoints in a variety of contexts.

This did not mean that the newspaper sugarcoated the news on these particular minorities after the events of 9/11; *Newsday* reported, as did the rest of the media, on organizations proved or suspected of channeling money to terrorist organizations, proved or alleged plots to commit anti-American terrorism, and similar revelations. Indeed, in the fall of 2005 *Newsday* broke the story of an imam, set to be officially sworn in as a New York City Fire Department chaplain, who told a reporter that he was not sure that the nineteen Arab and Muslim hijackers, Osama bin Laden, and Al Qaeda were responsible for the attacks of 9/11.[15] The page one story that was picked up by other news organizations caused such an uproar among firefighters— about one hundred of them Muslims—and among New Yorkers in general that Imam Intikab Habib withdrew immediately from the position. But although he expressed regrets that his publicized doubts about the identity of the 9/11 perpetrators had upset so many fellow New Yorkers, his statement not only cost him the $18,000 job but may have been damaging to the Muslim community as well. Speaking of the imam, one firefighter said, "His loyalty obviously doesn't lie with us, or with the United States."[16] While this incident could have unleashed a new virus of suspicion vis-à-vis Muslims in the region, *Newsday's* regular coverage of Muslim and Arab Americans' daily lives of normalcy was probably the best antidote for this.

In a six-month period from mid-March to mid-September 2005, *Newsday* published twenty-four items (articles, calendars, letters-to-the editor, etc.) that related to Muslims, Islam, and Long Island.[17] During the same period, there were thirty articles relating to either Muslim Americans or American Muslims on Long Island or elsewhere in the United States.[18] While these search words did not produce all relevant article summaries that reported on Muslim Americans or at least mentioned this minority, the results give us nevertheless a good idea of *Newsday's* practice of covering Muslim individuals and groups on Long Island and elsewhere frequently. Moreover, full articles from *Newsday's* pertinent coverage during the two-year period from July 2003 through July 2005 revealed what particular topics were featured, how well they informed readers on their Muslim compatriots, and to what extent Muslim Americans themselves were able to express their views.

"Waging Peace" was the headline on the full-page announcement of a lengthy and richly illustrated cover story in part 2 of a *Newsday* edition that reported on Imam Feisal Abdul Rauf and how he used his bully pulpit in New York City "to mend the relationship between the Islamic and Western worlds."[19] As reporter Carol Eisenberg put it, Imam Rauf's "ideas have been capturing the attention of leaders such as Rabbi David Rosen, international director of interreligious affairs for the American Jewish Committee; the Rev. George Carey, former archbishop of Canterbury, who chairs the international West-Islam dialogue group; and Queen Noor of Jordan." The writer offered the Imam ample opportunity to speak of his role and his aims in his own words. Describing himself as a mediator and bridge between the Islamic world and the West, Imam Rauf explained, "So, when I'm with Muslims, I tell them, 'Here are the things we have to do differently.' And when I'm with Christians and Jews, I say, 'Here are the things we have to do differently.'" What a far cry this story was from the frequent breaking news reports on yet another act of anti-Western terrorism abroad, hateful threats, and discovered terrorist plots.

Or take another multipage story that provided readers an understanding of African American Muslims and their strange predicament in the post–9/11 era. The lead paragraph referred to Imam Al-Hajj Talib Abdur-Rashid of the Mosque of the Islamic Brotherhood in Harlem, who "tells the story of a young African American Muslim who is asked what it's like living in post–Sept. 11 America. 'It's like being black,' he quotes him. 'Twice.'" The article described how the Muslim minority in New York and in America is not homogeneous but rather diverse and how "the divide between African American Muslims—a third of all American Muslims—and immigrants from South Asia and the Arab world has been significant." In poignant passages, the feature captured the emotions of Black Muslims and disseminated knowledge of the tradition of Islam among African Americans. Readers learned, for example, that contrary to conventional wisdom "only a few thousand of the estimated 2 million African American Muslims in America today belong to the Nation [of Islam led by Louis Farrakhan] since the conversion of Malcolm X in 1964 and of Warith Deen Mohammed in 1975." And Imam Abdur-Rashid was quoted as telling worshipers in his sermons, "Many of the people kidnapped to this country and sold into slavery were already Muslims."[20]

Another part 2 cover story, headlined "A Ramadan Release," was devoted to the first screening of the full-length animated feature film "Muhammad: The Last Prophet" at the end of Ramadan. While the article was written by a staff writer of the *Orlando Sentinel*, the Long Island newspaper featured it prominently. "What is a Muslim?" was the title of a lengthy and richly illustrated article that reported on young Muslims in New York City who were described as "part of an embryonic movement capturing the imagination of young Muslims across America, many of whom found each other in cyberspace."[21]

There was a long article on the seventy thousand or so Muslims on Long Island and their desire to practice their religion. According to the article,

> Life on Long Island presents a myriad of challenges to Muslims seeking to practice their faith. Only a handful of stores offer halal foods—meats and other products prepared according to Islamic religious law. With a handful of mosques scattered along the 90 miles from Elmont to Montauk, many Muslims live too far away to worship or socialize with fellow Muslims.[22]

The paper reported on the funeral of a young Muslim Long Islander who was killed in Iraq together with other scouts from the Army National Guard and was praised by his comrades as a great friend and great soldier.[23]

Newsday also covered Arab Americans living on Long Island and in the New York metropolitan area. Two years after 9/11, one article in particular described the grief and frustration of Arab Americans who lost loved ones in the terrorist attacks of 9/11 in a compelling way and the efforts of some Arab Americans to help. According to the report,

> Linda Sasour works 70 hours per week trying to reach an Arab-American community, which, she says, has been largely silent and frustrated since the Sept. 11 attacks. If recovery has been torturous for [non-Arab American] survivors and victims' families, it has been especially difficult for some Arab-Americans with few services to support their grief.[24]

But the same story noted as well that "[f]or some Arab-Americans . . . anti-Arab backlash, and the stress associated with it, is not an issue." One Arab American who lost his brother in the World Trade Center told the *Newsday* reporter that he "got support from people I knew and people I didn't."[25]

Perhaps even more important was the newspaper's habit to include Muslim and Arab organizations in its "Calendar" columns that listed the events of all kinds of organizations, to publish letters-to-the-editor from Muslim readers, and to ask members of the Muslim community for their views on all kinds of topics. Thus, following the bombings of the London transit system in July 2005, it published in its "faith questions" column under the headline "Asking Muslims: How should the world deal with Islamic terrorists?" the thoughtful answers of five Muslim Long Islanders to that question.[26] The same column publicized the views of the imam of a Harlem mosque along with the opinions of other religious leaders on the question, "Should religion play any role in the courtroom?"[27] On another occasion, when the question was whether it "is OK to bring religion to the office," the president of the Long Island Muslim Society was among those interviewed by a *Newsday* reporter.[28]

Since this was not a temporary reporting pattern but the quite regular coverage, this newspaper followed an approach of inclusion, since it covered Muslims and Arabs in the Long Island region as important parts of the multireligious, multiethnic, and multiracial makeup of a vibrant community—just like other minorities as well. No survey organization conducted public opinion polls on Long Island similar to those taken nationwide, and therefore it was impossible to determine whether people on Long Island had a better understanding of mainstream Muslim Americans than their compatriots across the nation. However, as the *New York Times* noted in a comprehensive story in the Long Island section of one of its Sunday editions in early September 2005,

> In truth, it appears that there has not been much trouble lately on Long Island. While scores of anti-Muslim incidents and hate crimes occurred in Nassau and Suffolk in the weeks immediately following 9/11, the police recorded only one minor case in each county last year: a vandalized car in Hicksville with an anti-Muslim note left on it, and a drunken commotion at a Stony Brook University dormitory, with shouted slurs and threats that led to two arrests. The trend is different, nationally, with the hate-crime rate up significantly in the last year [2004].[29]

While we cannot prove that the inclusive coverage of Muslim and Arab Americans in Long Island's *Newsday* affected the non-Muslim/non-Arab majority in this area and contributed to the absence of hate crimes, one would assume that the described reporting patterns helped readers to get to know Muslims and Arabs in their midst. Indeed, as the following exchange from a focus group session revealed, American Muslims recognized and pondered these reporting patterns:

Moderator: So [you say], *Newsday* is—is generally better balanced?

Male Voice: Oh, absolutely. It's—it's bizarre, it's so different from—from the [New York] *Daily News* and the [New York] *Post.* There was this, I think you might have all remembered this twenty-one-year old Pakistani who was missing after 9/11, and the people thought that he had something to do with—

Male Voice: Oh, yeah.

Male Voice: Something to do with the World Trade Center. But he was an EMS [Emergency Medical Services first responder] and he rushed down there.

Male Voice: Yeah. Yes.

Male Voice: And so, the day after his funeral, [Mayor] Bloomberg was there. It was at that big 96th Street mosque. It wasn't in any of the—it wasn't in the *Daily News,* it wasn't in the *Post,* and there it was on the cover, on the front page of *Newsday.* I—I mean, it just spoke volumes.

Moderator: Really? How—why is that?

Male Voice: You know, it's—I've been trying—thinking about it. I think this is their way of—of making themselves more unique. They're not going to—*Newsday* in this city is not going to compete with the *Daily News* or the *Post,* but they want it to be the smart, kind of second-read for people who read the *Times.* They don't want to go to the *Daily News* or the *Post.* But it is also owned by the company that happens to own the *Chicago Tribune* and the *L.A Times,* and those are communities with large Muslim populations. And they've lost a lot of white, suburban subscribers, and I think any paper that wants to survive now knows that they have to go after the immigrants to be their readers. And I—

Male Voice: Yes. Absolutely.

Male Voice: And I think that's probably in their—in the back of their minds as well.[30]

NOTES

1. The cartoon by Steve Benson was published in the *Arizona Republic* on July 31, 2005. See *www.azcentral.com/arizonarepublic/opinions/benson/articles/073105benso.html* (accessed August 8, 2005).

2. This cartoon was published in the *Arizona Republic* on July 28, 2005. See *www.azcentral/arizonarepublic/opinions/benson/articles/072805benson.html* (accessed August 8, 2005).

3. Paul Farhi, "WMAL suspends talk show host for comment on Islam," *Washington Post,* July 29, 2005, C1.

4. Paul Farhi, "Talk Show Host Graham Fired by WMAL over Islam Remarks," *Washington Post*, August 23, 2005, C1. The firing of Graham was a victory for the Council on American-Islam Relations, which had protested Graham's remarks. According to this *Washington Post* article, Graham was fired after he refused "to soften his description of Islam as 'a terrorist organization' on the air last month."

5. *Brian Lehrer Show*, WNYC, August 2, 2005.

6. *The O'Reilly Factor*, Fox News Network, July 28, 2005.

7. *News Hour with Jim Lehrer*, PBS, August 4, 2005.

8. Allie Shaw, "Those who accuse Muslims of silence, aren't listening very well," *Star Tribune* (Minneapolis), July 31, 2005, 1AA.

9. The text of the fatwa was published on the web site of the Council on American Islamic Relations, *www.cair.-net.org* (accessed August 3, 2005).

10. Laurie Goodstein, "From Muslims in America, a New Fatwa on Terrorism," *New York Times*, July 28, 2005, 14; Caryle Murphy, "U.S. Muslim Scholars to Forbid Terrorism," *Washington Post*, July 28, 2005, A11.

11. A search on LexisNexis that used the search words "fatwa," "Muslim," and "terrorism" produced fifty stories but only forty-three referred to the release of the fatwa discussed here.

12. According to press release by the Council on American-Islamic Relations on the organization's web site, *http://www.cair-net.org* (accessed August 8, 2005).

13. For the full text of these guidelines see *www.spj.org/diversity_profiling.asp* (accessed August 8, 2005).

14. We used the search words "Muslim American" and "American Muslim" to retrieve pertinent stories in the electronic LexisNexis archive.

15. Carol Eisenberg, "FDNY's 9/11 doubter," *Newsday*, September 30, A5.

16. Eisenberg, "FDNY's 9/11 doubter."

17. We picked this particular period because in the electronic LexisNexis archives *Newsday's* back issues are available only for the most recent six months.

18. We utilized the LexisNexis electronic archives for our search.

19. Carol Eisenberg, "Man in the Middle," *Newsday*, June 8, 2004, B1–B3, B10.

20. Carol Eisenberg, "An Islam rooted in America," *Newsday*, December 29, 2004, B2–B3.

21. Carol Eisenberg, "Toward a new Muslim moment," *Newsday*, October 20, 2004, B2–B3

22. Martin C. Evans, "Muslims try to find a common ground," *Newsday*, July 31, 2005, 22–23.

23. Wil Cruz, "Joined in mourning: Family and friends remember soldier in ceremonies that reflect both Muslim customs and military traditions," *Newsday*, March 19, 2005, A4.

24. Deborah S. Morris, "A Forgotten Community," *Newsday*, September 10, 2003, A24.

25. Morris, "A Forgotten Community."

26. Jim Smith, "Asking Muslims; How should the world deal with Islamic terrorists?" *Newsday*, July 16, 2005, B24.

27. Jim Merritt, "Asking the Clergy: Should religion play a role in the courtroom?" *Newsday*, July 9, 2005, B20.

28. Marcie Samartino, "Just Asking; Is it OK to bring religion to the office?" *Newsday*, July 23, 2005, B20.

29. Laurie Nadel, "Terrorist Attacks Committed in Islam's Name Fuel Fears and Widen Cultural Differences," *New York Times*, September 4, 2005, Section 14, 1 and 6.

30. This exchange occurred on June 11, 2003, during a focus group session with American Muslims who worked in the media.

3

The Visual Portrayal of Arabs and Muslims

Written words in newspapers and newsmagazines and spoken words in the electronic news media provide vast quantities of information. But visuals in the news—whether in the form of moving or still pictures—deserve just as much, or even more, attention because they tend to trigger the strongest cognitive and emotional effects in news consumers. Some eight decades ago, Walter Lippmann concluded that "[p]hotographs have the kind of authority over imagination to-day, which the printed word had yesterday, and the spoken word before that. They seem utterly real."[1] More recently, communication researchers found evidence that the recipients of news pay more attention to visual images than the spoken and written word, that readers and viewers become more engaged by pictures.[2] Moreover, as Doris Graber concluded, news consumers are more likely to recall visual than verbal messages.[3] People who watch television newscasts believe that pictures help them to understand the presented information.[4] This is particularly true in cases when the written or spoken words do not tell us—or do not tell us up front—about the ethnic or racial background of people in the news.

According to Martin Gilens, "the race of people pictured in news stories is a salient aspect of the story for many viewers."[5] Other researchers have found as well that the race of persons depicted in the news affected whether news consumers formed more positive or negative attitudes about the depicted people. Thus, Shanto Iyengar's laboratory experiments revealed that whites who watched virtually identical news stories about poor white and poor black people were likely to suggest that individual blacks needed to solve their predicaments themselves while suggesting societal solutions to help poor whites out of poverty. Given Iyengar's finding that "white, middle-class Americans" are "sensitive to skin color [of blacks depicted in TV news broadcasts]," it is likely that Westerners, including those in the United States, are also sensitive to the features and attire of Arabs and Muslims.[6]

To be sure, pictures do not always reveal the racial, ethnic, or religious backgrounds of the depicted persons, but in many instances visuals do convey the ethnic or racial background and sometimes, if only based on distinctive features of depicted persons' attire, the religious affiliations as well. Moreover, spoken words on broadcasts and written words in the print media sometimes provide information about persons shown in visuals that the pictures themselves do not provide.

While most communication researchers concentrate on television news when they examine the characteristics and influences of news images, we agree with Gilens's suggestion that pictures in the print media may have even greater impact than the fast-moving visuals on television screens. Gilens refers specifically to photographs in newsmagazines when he suggests that "even those who do not read a story are likely to look at least briefly at the picture as they browse through the magazine."[7] We believe that the same is true for visuals in daily newspapers—especially in the context of group identities. When news stories in the print press do not identify the race, ethnicity, or religion of people mentioned in the text, photographs do provide this information in many instances. Moreover, readers of newspapers, too, are likely to take note of photographs without choosing to read the news stories these pictures illustrate; they may read the captions, if they see compelling photographs and seek more information.

If we assume that a picture in the news is worth a thousand words and that viewers and readers react to the ethnic, racial, and religious group membership of depicted persons, content analyses of the media are incomplete without thorough examinations of the visual images. As Cori Dauber concluded, "In an increasingly media-saturated environment, ignoring visual imagery provides less and less satisfactory work."[8] Moreover, "the examination of print media lacks something critical when accompanying photographs, much less layout and other aspects of graphic design, are ignored."[9]

For all of these reasons, we conducted a detailed analysis of several thousand visuals in the daily and weekly print press and in a limited number of national and local TV newscasts. (The appendix contains a more detailed description of our research considerations and methodology.)

VISUALS IN *NEWSWEEK* AND *TIME* MAGAZINES

Just as daily newspapers in the New York area and across the United States devoted few news stories and pictures to Muslims and Arabs in the United States in the six months before 9/11, *Newsweek* and *Time* were no exception to this predominant trend. Thus, only a total of nine such photographs were published in the two newsmagazines in the half year preceding 9/11. In the six months following the 9/11 attacks the two publications combined carried 76 pictures of Arabs and Muslims in the United States. The contrast between the pre- and post-9/11 periods was even more pronounced with respect to visuals that showed Arabs and Muslims abroad: Whereas the two newsmagazines published a total of 32 such photographs before the attacks in New York and Washington, they carried 377 visuals of this kind afterward. Of the few pictures of Muslims and Arabs in the United States published in *Newsweek*, our coders deemed 40 percent as conveying negative messages while they saw 60 percent as neutral or ambiguous. *Time*, on the other hand, carried more images painting members of these groups in a positive light (50 percent); coders perceived the rest as fitting the negative (25 percent) or neutral/ambiguous (25 percent) categories. But the small number of relevant pictures does not allow meaningful conclusions as to the photo editors' choices during this period or useful comparisons between the pre- and post-9/11 periods. Yet, in terms of sheer number of published photographs, the difference was significant. More importantly, in the six months after the attacks on the World Trade Center and the Pentagon, *Newsweek*'s visual depictions of Muslims and Arabs in the United States were deemed by our coders to be more positive than negative whereas those in *Time* magazine were evaluated as more negative than positive.

When Americans in New York or elsewhere in the United States receive the news, whether in the form of pictures or written and spoken words, or both, they probably do not distinguish strictly and consciously between members of particular groups in their own community, their own country, or abroad—particularly not when the news receivers consider such groups as threatened, oppressed, threatening, or otherwise problematic. For this reason, we included pictures that depicted Arabs and Muslims abroad in this part of our analysis as well.

Of the small number of pictures of Muslims and Arabs abroad published in the pages of *Newsweek* in the six months preceding the 9/11 bombings, the overwhelming majority (70 percent) were perceived by our coders to depict members of these groups in a negative light; 20 percent were evaluated as neutral or ambiguous; only 10 percent were judged to be sympathetic or positive. Carrying more than twice as many pertinent visuals than *Newsweek* during this period, *Time* magazine, too, showed Muslims and Arabs outside the United States far more often in negative or unsympathetic ways (46 percent) than as sympathetic figures (8 percent), while a large number of these images seemed neutral or ambiguous. As expected, both newsmagazines carried far more pertinent photographs in the six months following September 11, 2001, and far more of those conveyed negative messages with respect to the shown Muslims or Arabs abroad than positive or sympathetic ones.

We found our comprehensive qualitative analysis of the photographs published in *Newsweek* and *Time* far more revealing because this method allowed us to trace patterns in the selection of visuals that were not obvious when we simply categorized large quantities of pictures along the positive-neutral-negative scale. First of all, we established similarities in the pre- and post-9/11 visuals in that the vast majority of them illustrated stories about Muslims and Arabs at home and abroad, mostly in the context of terrorism or counterterrorism and in connection with the conflict between Israelis and Palestinians. Thus, Osama bin Laden's picture was published twice in *Newsweek* during the six months preceding 9/11—once as the smiling éminence grise behind the suicide bombing of the USS *Cole* in the fall of 2000; the other time as terrorist mastermind stirring fears of new anti-American attacks.[10] *Time*, too, illustrated a story about the USS *Cole* investigation with a picture of bin Laden. And there was a photograph of Iraq's president Saddam Hussein along with a story that described his support for Palestinian terrorists involved in fighting and killing Israelis.[11] More prominently placed were the large and colored portraits of two prominent Hezbollah and Hamas leaders, Sheik Hassan Nasrallah and Khaled al-Masha'al. The huge headline that separated their photographs on top of a two-page story spread identified the two men as "The Terror Twins" (with the word "Terror" printed in red) and stated furthermore, "The Middle East's most violent terrorists have been in competition to outdo each other. Now they're allying."[12] A cover story on the roots of evil that took the soon-to-be-executed Oklahoma City bomber Timothy McVeigh as a starting point was accompanied by a picture of Ramzi Yousef, the mastermind of the first World Trade Center bombing in 1993. Yousef was identified as one of the evil "zealots" along with the "Unabomber," Theodore Kaczynski, whose picture was shown as well. Interestingly, of the nine pictures of Muslims in the American domestic context in *Time* and *Newsweek*, three showed the terrorist mastermind Ramzi Yousef, who was serving a life sentence in a federal prison in Colorado and was not then and is not now a U.S. citizen and thus not a Muslim American.

Pictures of the predominant Middle East problem typically depicted Palestinian women as suffering and mourning, while male Palestinians were shown as defiant, militant, and threatening. *Newsweek*, for example, published the heart-wrenching picture of a Palestinian mother mourning her son who was killed by Israeli soldiers.[13] Another photograph showed a Palestinian mother with head scarf holding her baby as she stood at an Israeli checkpoint with Israeli soldiers nearby. This visual illustrated the same story that was also accompanied by a huge picture spanning one and one-half pages of what the caption described as "Fatah militants at the funeral of a 15-year-old killed by the Israelis." With their fingers on the triggers of Kalashnikov rifles, the masked men looked not like mourners but rather like menacing aggressors.[14] *Time* seemed particularly inclined to publish the pictures

of Palestinian boys in scenes and activities that demonstrated their early devotion to violence for the Palestinian cause. Thus, in one of these visuals a
young boy in what looked like army fatigues kissed the portrait of Abu Ali
Mustafa, a leader of the Popular Front for the Liberation of Palestine, who
had been assassinated by Israelis.[15] On another occasion, the same magazine
displayed the picture of a young boy who carried a fake suicide belt around
his waist holding a cord in his hand as if he was ready to ignite the explo-
sives and die for the cause. The caption stated, "CHILDREN'S CRUSADE: At
a parade last week, a young Palestinian in costume."[16]

Ironically, the image of the boy outfitted like a suicide bomber accompanied a story about the exploitation of visual images by both Israelis and
Palestinians in order to document the other side's violence. According to
the text, "Every photograph tells the truth." But the ultimate point was that
powerful images reflect one reality—the truth of one side. Strangely, to illustrate this thoughtful examination of what the headline summarized as
"The Struggle Over Spin: Trading Shots, Trading Snapshots," the editors selected this shocking picture of a Palestinian child playing suicide bomber—
without commenting on the reason for this choice. Was this spin on the
part of the photographer? Was it the editors' intent to show a picture that
exemplified spin? If so, it was not at all clear, certainly not for the hurried
reader who just skimmed the pages and was likely to take notice only of the
most compelling visuals. *Time* showed Muslim women several times as the
victims of violence. For example, the face of a young woman dominated a
picture shot at the mass funeral for Muslims killed nearly ten years earlier
in Bosnia.[17] And there was the Muslim Albanian mother with her two sons
shown after a shell hit her house during the civil war in Macedonia.[18]

In spite of the altogether scarce coverage of Arabs and Muslims at home
and abroad in the months before 9/11, *Newsweek* devoted a whole page to
the horror story of an Iranian man who had brutally killed at least sixteen
prostitutes and who was reportedly considered a hero by conservative Muslims in his homeland. The story was illustrated with pictures of the killer
and his victims.[19] If news reporting from Iran and other Muslim countries
had been frequent and comprehensive during this period, one would not
wonder about the selection of this crime story for publication. But because
the overall coverage was spotty and one-dimensional, the overall visual depiction of Muslims and Arabs came close to what Edward Said characterized
two decades earlier as "essentialized caricatures of the Islamic world."[20]

MORE—BUT THE SAME TYPES OF VISUALS AFTER 9/11

While the quantity of pertinent pictures was significantly larger after 9/11,
the predominant motives and images of the depicted Muslims in the

United States and abroad did not change in comparison to the previous period. In the ten weeks following the attacks of 9/11, *Time* magazine depicted
Osama bin Laden three times on its cover, *Newsweek* two times. While the
covers of these two leading newsmagazines always command a great deal of
attention, they were in these particular cases only the tip of the iceberg as
far as the magazine's visuals of bin Laden, his Al Qaeda lieutenants and followers, his Taliban allies, and the 9/11 perpetrators and co-conspirators
were concerned.

Take, for example, the first regular issue that *Time* published after the
events of 9/11: The cover shows the now famous picture of President
George W. Bush at Ground Zero in New York, surrounded by firemen and
other rescue workers waving an American flag.[21] The inside pages carry
many pictures of the incredible devastation, the victims, the rescuers—several of these images filling two pages each. And then there are the huge facial close-ups of the architect-in-chief and the perpetrators of the suicide attacks—one whole page of bin Laden's face, close-up pictures looking like
mug shots of Mohammed Atta and Marwan al-Shehhi, two of the Arab men
aboard the hijacked jetliners, each visual filling two-thirds of a page. The
same photographs, albeit in smaller sizes, are shown on the following
pages. There are two pictures of the same smiling bin Laden at the wedding
of his son—one showing him with family members, the other—an obvious
excerpt of the first picture—depicting him alone. Finally, there are several
pictures of Al Qaeda's rank-and-file followers and of Taliban members.

To be sure, *Time*, like other newsmagazines, daily newspapers, and, of
course, television networks and stations, used these kinds of pictures and
similar ones to piece together the horror story of 9/11. This was simply
good reporting on an event that had an immediate and lasting impact on
the United States and the rest of the world. Yet, the superlarge and redun-
dant facial close-ups of bin Laden and the suicide bombers in his service
amplified the impact of these threatening visuals. Research has revealed
that visual depictions of human beings—and especially facial close-ups—
are especially resonant and memorable.[22] And because pictures of dramatic,
tragic, violent scenes are particularly effective in getting the attention of and
being remembered especially well by news consumers, the scenes of devastation and of victims next to the large-looming facial close-ups of bin Laden
and his followers magnified the moral gap between the innocent victims of
the 9/11 carnage and the perpetrators and masterminds behind the attack.

Given the magnitude of the attacks and their consequences, nobody
would question the magazine's choice to publish these images. But other
important images that could have contributed to a better understanding between the Muslim and Arab minorities and the non-Muslim majority in the
United States were mostly ignored in this crucial issue after the attacks.
With the exception of a relatively small picture on page 39 that showed

three Muslim women in Florida mourning the victims of 9/11, *Time* did not illustrate the predicament of Muslim and Arab Americans during these most difficult days and thereby missed the opportunity to show its readers that terrorists are the exception, not the rule, among Muslims and Arabs in their midst.

In this respect *Newsweek* offered a far more balanced selection of visual images in its first issue after 9/11. To be sure, there were the traumatic shots of the burning and falling twin towers, of heroic rescuers at Ground Zero, of victims and their loved ones, of mourning people all around the country. And there were the cold faces of the attackers—Mohammed Atta and Marwan al-Shehhi—and of Osama bin Laden aiming his AK-47 at an invisible target. But none of these images filled more than a quarter of a page. And in sharp contrast to *Time*, *Newsweek*'s editors devoted a full page to the anguished face of a Muslim American woman in Florida, who, according to the caption, "worries outside a Muslim school."[23] Under the headline "A Peaceful Faith, A Fanatic Few," an article on the following page was illustrated with two more photographs of Muslims and Arabs: the first showed Muslim worshipers in a mosque in New Jersey, the second depicted an Arab American Muslim father and his young son, an American flag in hand, on their way to give blood for the victims of 9/11.[24] Finally, there was the picture of Hasson Awahd, an Arab American, who was the target of a violent "revenge attack" in the aftermath of the terrorist attacks.[25] There is no doubt, then, that unlike *Time*, *Newsweek* offered readers in its first issue after 9/11 a selection of visuals that depicted Arabs and Muslims abroad and at home in a more balanced way—the bad and the good.

In its October 1 issue, the second after 9/11, *Time* devoted a three-page spread to "Muslims, Sikhs and Arabs" described as "patriotic, integrated— and growing." The text was illustrated by photographs of Sikhs, among them a turbaned man wrapped in an American flag, a mourning Muslim American student, and American Muslims, Sikhs, and Coptic Christians who were the victims of hate crimes across the country immediately after 9/11.[26] But these images were overshadowed by the portrait of bin Laden on the cover, three other photographs of the Al Qaeda leader inside the magazine, and a multitude of visuals of the 9/11 hijackers and of Taliban guerillas. *Newsweek*, in its second issue after 9/11, carried a superclose and obviously digitally manipulated facial close-up shot of bin Laden on its cover and another full-page picture of the Al Qaeda boss inside the magazine. There were also pictures of several of the 9/11 hijackers, and of Taliban soldiers and of "angry 'students' of the Faith" in Afghanistan who, according to the caption, "put women in purdah and arrest Christians for teaching their beliefs."[27] Finally, readers were exposed to the images of catastrophic pre-9/11 terrorist attacks committed by Al Qaeda or related groups—the Khobar Towers bombing in Saudi Arabia in 1996 as well as the attacks on the U.S. embassies in East Africa in 1998 and the USS *Cole* in 2000. Unlike *Newsweek*'s edition of the previous week, this issue was devoid of visual reminders that not all Muslims and Arabs are religious fanatics and terrorists.

Apart from the huge number of visuals that showed terrorists, such as the 9/11 hijackers, bin Laden, his Al Qaeda associates, and members of other terrorist groups, Muslim males in general were overwhelmingly depicted as terrorists, suspected terrorists, sympathizers of terrorist groups, or otherwise utterly evil. Muslim women, on the other hand, were once again mostly shown as victims of all kinds of conflicts and in many cases as battered by Muslim males. The negative depiction of Muslim males was especially pronounced in the context of the Afghanistan war. *Time* magazine's issue of November 26, 2001, exemplified this tendency. As part of a twelve-page photo-essay readers were presented with a two-page pictorial spread that consisted of a five-photograph sequence on "vengeance."

- The first photograph shows fighters of the Northern Alliance (allied with the United States–led coalition forces) who retrieve an injured Taliban soldier from a ditch where he probably was hiding.
- In the second picture, the Northern Alliance fighters drag the wounded Taliban to the road.
- The next scene shows the injured man pleading for his life.
- The fourth visual is a close-up of the Taliban soldier's frightened face. According to the caption, he is begging for mercy.
- The final, most gruesome picture proves that his pleas are in vain: The Northern Alliance fighters shoot him several times and kill him.

Nobody would question the brutality of war and the need for visuals that convey the harsh reality of military conflicts and related atrocities. But this pictorial story was less about the horror of war than about the brutality and inhumanity of Afghan men—Muslim men. It was utterly unlikely that those who viewed these and similar pictures felt any compassion for the victim, because he was identified as a Taliban soldier and thus tagged as no less brutal than his killers. After all, many of the post-9/11 pictures illustrated how male-dominated Muslim societies and individual Muslim men—especially the Taliban—committed violence, even against their own women.

Many of these visuals depicted abused females in Afghanistan. *Newsweek*, for example, illustrated a story on the "deeply ambivalent role women play in bin Laden's world" with a picture of an Afghan man beating a woman during the Taliban rule.[28] *Time* carried a one-and-one-third-page picture spread of abused women—one depicting the public whipping of Afghan women by males. Another horrifying photograph showed a fifteen-year-old female in a Peshawar shelter with severe burns. According to the caption, she was thus punished by her father-in-law for not properly cleaning her husband's clothes.[29] And then there was the *Newsweek* cover story "Married to Al Qaeda. The American Wife of a bin Laden Operative: A Journey into Jihad."[30] Although the story described April Ray as not fitting "the stereotype of the meek and submissive Islamic fundamentalist wife [a stereotype that the mass media, ironically, cultivates]" and as "feisty and at times cagey as she sought to prove her husband's innocence," the pictures of the thirty-four-year-old mother of seven children in long dress and head scarf most likely triggered mixed reactions among readers of *Time* magazine: On the one hand they must have felt disbelief that a woman, born and raised in the U.S., could have been unaware of her husband's Al Qaeda ties; on the other hand they may have felt sympathy for one more Muslim female suffering because of a male Muslim. It was a variation of the common theme except that this time around the suffering woman was an American convert to Islam.

If one believes the visual images presented in these publications, most Muslim boys are eager to follow in the "evil" footsteps of their fathers while little girls get early on a bitter taste of the female predicament in Muslim societies. The many pictures that depicted suffering Muslim children showed mostly, often exclusively, little girls.[31] Just as in the pre-9/11 period, the pictures of boys fit the mold of the threatening Muslim male. The most glaring example was *Newsweek's* cover of October 15, 2001, that showed a serious little boy, his finger on the trigger of a toy gun, at an anti-American rally in Islamabad, Pakistan. One wonders why this photograph was chosen to alert readers to the cover story by Fareed Zakaria titled "Why They Hate Us: The Roots of Islamic Rage—And What We Can Do About It."

NEWSWEEK AND *TIME*—ONE YEAR AFTER 9/11

In their editions of September 11, 2002, as one would expect, both *Newsweek* and *Time* covered the first anniversary of 9/11 with commemorative cover stories and a multitude of touching and, no doubt, appropriate photographs of the devastated sites, the victims, family members, and rescuers. There were also images of bin Laden in both magazines, of several suspected 9/11 plotters (*Newsweek*), and five of bin Laden's lieutenants (*Time*) as well as several shots of the youthful 9/11 hijacker-in-chief Mohammed Atta, his father, and his sisters (*Time*). In the other issues published in September 2002, *Time*, far more than *Newsweek*, published many pictures of "Islamic" terrorists—most of them said to be tied to the Al Qaeda network. Accompanying a cover story ("Confessions of an Al-Qaeda Terrorist") in its September 23 edition, *Time* magazine published more than a dozen pictures of Al Qaeda terrorists. But unlike a year earlier, there were no images of (and no stories about) Muslims and Arabs in America that would have reminded readers that members of these religious and ethnic groups had nothing in common with the bin Ladens of this world. There were, however, several pictures of Saddam Hussein—both magazines published one that showed the Iraqi president aggressively holding a saber—among them visuals that illustrated cover stories ("Target: Iraq; The War over War" in *Newsweek*; "Are We Ready For War?" in *Time*) on the intensifying Washington-Baghdad conflict. As the Bush administration moved toward the invasion of Iraq, the images of Saddam Hussein seemed to overtake Osama bin Laden in the pictorial "contest" for the title of evildoer-in-chief.

Once again, the newsmagazines displayed the contrast between the overwhelmingly negative images of male Muslims and Arabs of all ages and the sympathetic or at least value-neutral depictions of Muslim or Arab females. *Time*, for example, carried the picture of an Afghan woman who had been the highest-ranking female member of the Afghan Air Force before the rule of the Taliban and who was able to make the switch from burqa to beret after the victory of the American-led coalition forces. Another picture depicted the veiled wife of an Al Qaeda terrorist who said, according to the caption, that she had no knowledge about her husband's activities.[32]

In sum, then, stereotypes continued to dominate with respect to the visuals selected by the two newsmagazines for publication in that the depicted males were most likely terrorists or otherwise evil threats, in sharp contrast to the sympathetic depiction of females.

As far as we can tell, all of these visuals were genuine and not staged for the benefit of photographers or chosen by editors to magnify the negative male and the sympathetic female stereotypes. But this selection projected only part of the reality in the lives and activities of Muslims in the United States and abroad. In the post-9/11 climate of shock and fear, even the media's own ethics rules with regard to visual images were at times disregarded. Thus, a full-page, heavily red-tinted facial shot of bin Laden was published in *Time's* first post-9/11 issue that magnified the Al Qaeda leader's personification of evil and corresponded to President Bush's characterization of bin Laden as evildoer.[33] The same picture—without the hellish tint—appeared on the cover of the newsmagazine's next issue.[34] People inside the media tend to be very critical when they detect the deliberate alteration of a visual image—as was the case when *Time* darkened the mug shot of O. J. Simpson after he was accused of murdering his wife in 1994.[35] Addressing the *Time*-Simpson controversy, Bill Steigerwald of the *Pittsburgh Post-Gazette* warned at the time that "messing with news reality is the most serious mortal sin in journalism, which is why *Time* has been catching hell all week."[36] The managing editor of the *Buffalo News*, Murray B. Light, wrote, "Long before *Time* magazine altered O. J. Simpson's police mug shot on the cover of its June 27 issue, newsrooms throughout the country were acutely aware of the possible abuses that could arise with the advent of electronic imaging in the process of editing news photographs."[37] Assuring the readers of the *News* that the Buffalo paper adhered strictly to the Associated Press's photo ethics code that prohibits any alteration of photographs, Light stated furthermore,

> In light of the Simpson-Time incident, it is important to note that the photo ethics code also states that "serious consideration must always be given in correcting color to ensure honest reproduction of the original. Cases of abnormal color or tonality will be clearly stated in the caption. Color adjustment should always be minimal."[38]

These ethics rules were violated when the newsmagazine "enhanced" the portrait of bin Laden by tinting it red. Although this was not a minimal alteration, there was no criticism. Obviously, nobody felt that journalistic values mattered when the photograph of the suspected mastermind of the 9/11 horrors was involved. Yet, however strongly many Americans may have wished for bin Laden to go to hell in the face of the unprecedented terrorist attack, the media and other institutions must uphold fundamental values and ethics, especially in the face of major crises. Otherwise terrorists can rightly claim, as bin Laden did after 9/11, that Western democracies, led by the United States, abandon their declared values when they face a serious threat.

DAILY NEWSPAPERS AND VISUALS OF MUSLIMS AND ARABS

As described in chapter 1, the post-9/11 portrayal of Muslim and Arab Americans in newspaper stories was more positive than negative. But the visual depiction of members of these minorities was significantly more negative than positive in three of the four newspapers we examined. As table 3.1 demonstrates, the *New York Times* was the only one of the four publications that published far more sympathetic than unsympathetic images of these minorities.

Taken together, then, unsympathetic or negative depictions of Arabs and Muslims in the United States, who were often alleged to be terrorists, supporters of terrorists, or simply critical of governmental reactions to the attacks of 9/11, outnumbered the images of those who mourned the victims of 9/11, helped in the recovery efforts, or were shown as victims of hate crimes or unjust counterterrorist measures. This negative trend survived into the weeks before and after the first 9/11 anniversary in the *Daily News*, the *Post*, and in *USA Today*. And, unlike in the months immediately following the 9/11 attacks, the *New York Times* was no longer an exception but in a complete turnaround published mostly negative visuals.

Only a relatively small number of photographs illustrated local events, developments, or conditions that involved Muslims and Arabs in the New

Table 3.1 Depictions of Arabs and Muslims in the United States: Visuals in Daily Newspapers in the Six Months after 9/11

	NY Times	NY Daily News	NY Post	USA Today
	(%)	(%)	(%)	(%)
Positive	14	10	3	8
Probl. Positive	29	6	3	9
Neutral/Ambig.	42	39	65	48
Probl. Negative	10	10	12	25
Negative	5	35	17	10
	N=160	N=80	N=120	N=79

N = Number of visuals
Source: Muslims in New York City Project

York metro area in the six months after 9/11. It is noteworthy, however, that the photographs published in the three New York newspapers added up to a portrayal of Muslims and Arabs that was far more positive than negative. However, this trend did not survive for long. Around the time of the first 9/11 anniversary, two of the newspapers published significantly more unsympathetic than sympathetic images, while the share of negative visuals increased in the third paper. In short, by the time the first 9/11 anniversary came around, the visual images of Muslim and Arab Americans in the local New York setting were almost equally as unsympathetic as those published in the national news context.

DAILY NEWSPAPERS:
VISUALS OF ARABS AND MUSLIMS ABROAD

Far more Arabs and Muslims abroad were pictured in the six months after 9/11 (a total of 1,846 in the four publications combined) than Arabs and Muslims inside the United States (a total of 439). With the exception of *USA Today*, which carried a slightly larger percentage of positive than negative images, the other three newspapers published more negative than positive visuals. But at the same time and surprisingly, three of the four publications (*USA Today*, the *New York Post*, and the *New York Daily News*) also selected a larger percentage of sympathetic photographs of Arabs and Muslims abroad than of members of these minorities in the domestic American setting. The single most important factor here was the pictorial depiction of Palestinian victims in the violent conflict between Israelis and Palestinians in early

2002 that coders deemed in many instances as invoking sympathy for Arabs and Muslims shown as victims of Israel's military actions in response to a wave of lethal suicide bombings.

In the weeks before and after the first anniversary of 9/11, however, the photographic depictions of Arabs and Muslims abroad were significantly more negative than in the half year after the terrorist attacks. This negative trend was especially pronounced in the *New York Post*, where two-thirds of these visuals were deemed to be unsympathetic or negative versus only about one-third in the six months after 9/11, and in *USA Today*, where the proportion of negative visuals jumped from one-fourth to nearly two-thirds.

Contrary to our expectations, we did not find significant differences in the pictorial depictions of Muslims and Arabs in the United States on the one hand and of members of these religious and ethnic groups abroad on the other.

FROM PARTIAL REALITY TOWARD
A MORE COMPLETE PICTURE

In the fall of 2005, when U.S. Assistant Secretary of State Karen Hughes took charge of the Bush administration's public diplomacy efforts in the Muslim and Arab world and embarked on an initial "listening trip" to Egypt, Saudi Arabia, and Turkey, Muslim women in Saudi Arabia in particular complained about the stereotypical depiction of Muslims in the American media—the male as violent and the female as oppressed. Our qualitative and quantitative content analyses of visuals confirmed the dominance of images that these Muslim and Arab women complained about. To be sure, during the periods we focused on, a great deal of the day-to-day news was about Muslims and Arabs who had committed or threatened terrorism against the United States, the West, and Israel or were reportedly suspected of training for and plotting terrorist attacks. As a result, the media publicized many visuals that depicted Muslims, mostly males, as killers and would-be killers of innocents. These images were part of the day-in and day-out reporting on the major news events at the time and thus part of the free media's responsibility to inform the public. But taken together, these pictures reflected only the most dramatic, threatening, sensational, and shocking excerpts of the whole reality and left out the full range of Muslims' peaceful, lawful, and perfectly normal existence. There is reason to believe that such lopsided images, along with the reporting patterns we described in the previous chapters, affected how members of the Muslim minority and the non-Muslim majority in America viewed and related to each other. As Walter Lippmann recognized more than eighty years ago, "The subtlest and most pervasive of all influences are those which create and maintain a repertory of stereotypes."[39]

This one-sidedness in media images was reminiscent of the way the news depicted black American communities in the past and, to a lesser extent, still does today. Following widespread and deadly riots in predominantly black inner cities in the 1960s, the National Commission on Civil Disorders, also known as the Kerner Commission, found an array of problems in the reporting patterns of these disturbances, for example, that too much coverage was devoted to "emotional events" and to African American "militant" leaders' roles in stirring up violence.[40] But the most important criticism was reserved for the media's failure to reflect a comprehensive picture of the African American minority. As the Kerner Commission stated at the time, "By failing to portray the Negro [this was the term used at the time] as a matter of routine and in the context of the total society, the news media have, we believe, contributed to the black-white schism in this country."[41] We found this same incompleteness in the visual portrayal of Muslims and Arabs in the United States—and overseas as well. Just as news media of the past depicted Black Americans as if they didn't live a normal life and, in the words of the Kerner Commission, "give birth, marry, die, and go to PTA meetings,"[42] news organizations have similarly failed to fully portray the normalcy of Muslims in America (and of Muslims and Arabs abroad as well).

This should not be standard operating procedure, as the *New York Times* demonstrated on three consecutive days in early March 2006 with the publication of an unusual selection of large and prominently placed photographs that illustrated a series of in-depth articles about the life and work of the imam of a Muslim congregation in the Bay Ridge section of Brooklyn, New York.[43] When the first installment of the series by Andrea Elliott with photographs by James Estrin was published, the paper's front page carried above the fold a large photograph of Sheik Reda Shata, the Brooklyn imam, in a traditional white robe and nearly touched by a large American flag on the sidewalk. In spite of the local character of the series, all three parts were placed on the front pages and continued in the national, not metropolitan New York sections. This was the right placement decision because the bulk of the news about Muslims and Arabs is driven by national and international events, developments, and conditions—not by local occurrences. When these excellent articles and photographs were published, the news of the day happened to include the visual images of the would-be 9/11 terrorist Zacharias Moussaoui before and during his trial's sentencing phase, of Muslim protesters raging against the United States during President Bush's visit to India and Pakistan, of Saddam Hussein's outbursts in a Baghdad court, and of all kinds of violent attacks by Muslims in Afghanistan, Iraq, and elsewhere. Again, there was nothing wrong with the media's airing and printing these and similarly disconcerting images. But by publishing pictures of the everyday life of one imam and his flock along with extensive text reportage (and additional videotapes on the newspaper's web site)—the imam blessing a newborn baby, conducting a wedding ceremony, pondering the pros and cons of a divorce request, acting as matchmaker, accompanying his children to school, or riding the subway in Western clothes—the *Times* focused this time around on depicting the generally ignored normal human activities, the joys and the sorrows that are common to all human beings and all communities regardless of their religious, racial, and ethnic makeup.

Nearly forty years ago, the Kerner Commission warned that the white American, if conditioned by the media's incomplete portrayal of Black America, would "neither understand nor accept the black American."[44] In the ongoing "war on terrorism" climate and its focus on "the ugly Muslim," one could similarly argue that an incomplete mass-mediated picture of Muslims in America prevents the non-Muslim American from understanding and accepting the Muslim American. Unless the media publish more often images of the everyday lives of Muslims in America.

NOTES

1. Walter Lippmann, *Public Opinion* (1922; repr. New York: Free Press, 1997), 61.

2. See, for example, Russel W. Neumann, Marion Just, and Ann N. Crigler, *Common Knowledge* (Chicago: University of Chicago Press, 1992).

3. Doris Graber, "Seeing is Remembering: How Visuals Contribute to Learning from Television News," *Journal of Communication* 40 (1997): 134–55.

4. Neumann et al., 55–58.

5. Martin Gilens, "Race and Poverty in America: Public Misperceptions and the American News Media," *Public Opinion Quarterly* 60, no. 4 (1996): 528.

6. Shanto Iyengar, *Is Anyone Responsible?* (Chicago: University of Chicago Press, 1991), 67, 68. Based on his experiments, Iyengar determined that people use race as a "contextual tool" when thinking about certain problems and policy issues, most of all poverty.

7. Gilens, "Race and Poverty in America," n. 13.

8. Cori E. Dauber, "The Shots seen 'round the World: The Impact of the Images of Mogadishu on American Military Operations," *Rhetoric and Public Affairs* 4, no. 4 (2001): 655.

9. Dauber, "The Shots seen 'round the World."

10. Bin Laden's photographs appeared in *Newsweek*'s issues of March 26, 2001, 39; and July 30, 2001, 6.

11. *Time*, August 27, 2001, 31.

12. *Time*, April 30, 2001, 38, 39.

13. *Newsweek*, July 9, 2001, 42.

14. *Newsweek,* June 11, 2001, 20–23.

15. *Time,* September 10, 2001, 40, 41.

16. *Time,* April 9, 2001, 58.

17. *Time,* August 6, 2001, 30.

18. *Time,* April 2, 2001, 30.

19. *Newsweek,* August 20, 2001, 28.

20. Edward W. Said, *Covering Islam: How the Media and the Experts Determine how we see the Rest of the World* (New York: Pantheon Books, 1981), 26.

21. *Time,* September 24, 2001.

22. Graber, "Seeing is Remembering," 137–39.

23. *Newsweek,* September 24, 2001, 66.

24. *Newsweek,* September 24, 2001, 67, 68.

25. *Newsweek,* September 24, 2001, 69.

26. *Time,* October 1, 2001, 72–74.

27. *Newsweek,* October 1, 2001, 32.

28. *Newsweek,* January 14, 2002, 48.

29. *Time,* December 3, 2001, 40, 41.

30. *Newsweek,* Janary 14, 2002, 40ff.

31. See, for example, "Photo Essay: War as a Way of Life," *Time,* November 5, 2001, 60, 61.

32. *Time,* September 16, 2002, 38.

33. *Time,* September 24, 2001, 55.

34. *Time,* October 1, 2001.

35. For the controversial cover, see *Time,* June 27, 1994.

36. Bill Steigerwald, "TIME Steps Over Line by Altering O. J. Picture," *Pittsburgh Post-Gazette,* June 23, 1994, C1.

37. Murray B. Light, "TIME Sacrifices Ethics in Altering Simpson Photo," *Buffalo News,* June 29, 1994.

38. Light, "TIME Sacrifices Ethics."

39. Lippmann, *Public Opinion,* 59.

40. National Commission on Civil Disorders, *Report of the National Commission on Civil Disorders* (New York: The New York Times Company, 1968), 364.

41. National Commission on Civil Disorders, *Report,* 383.

42. National Commission on Civil Disorders, *Report,* 383.

43. Andrea Elliott, "An Imam in America," with photographs by James Estrin, appeared in the *New York Times* on March 5, 6, and 7, 2006.

44. National Commission on Civil Disorders, *Report,* 383.

4

How Americans View Islam and Muslims at Home and Abroad

More than eighty years ago, when newspapers were the public's predominant sources of political information, the press was central in Walter Lippmann's observation on the formation and nature of public opinion. Recognizing that much of what people know about the world around them is not based on personal experience but on secondhand information, Lippmann mentioned newspaper stories and photographs in particular as shaping the pictures in our heads. Nothing has changed in this respect—except that radio, television, and the Internet joined the print media as information sources that influence public perceptions and convey or reinforce the persistent stereotypes that have deep roots in the dominant cultural traditions. Even when reporters, editors, producers, and others in the news media consciously reject stereotypes of racial, ethnic, and religious minorities, as many do, they may still react subconsciously in accordance with enduring stereotypes as Martin Gilens found with respect to the stereotypical selection of African American visuals in the news.[1]

The textual and pictorial news coverage of Muslim Americans, Muslims abroad, and the religion of Islam that we described in the previous three chapters confirmed Walter Lippmann's recognition that the news is utterly incomplete and, as he put it, "like the beam of a searchlight that moves restlessly about, bringing one episode and then another out of the darkness into vision."[2] But the news media are not the only suppliers of interpretive frames that affect people's attitudes and perceptions, optimism and pessimism, hopes and fears. Entertainment, such as motion pictures, television shows, pop music, and advertising, contributes to people's sentiments as well. Researchers found this to be the case with respect to the predominant black images in the American news, entertainment, and advertising media and white Americans' views on African Americans.[3] Similarly, except for a minority of non-Muslim Americans who are acquainted with fellow Muslims and thus can draw on personal experiences, Americans' views of Muslims at home and abroad and the religion of Islam are most of all shaped by the totality of various types of mass-mediated descriptions and images. It is actually difficult to assess how many non-Muslim Americans do have Muslim relatives, friends, or acquaintances. Three weeks after 9/11, 41 percent of respondents claimed to know someone who is Muslim, but five months later only 28 percent said that they were acquainted with a Muslim.

Assessing the impact of the media's portrayal of Blacks on Whites in America, Robert M. Entman and Andrew Rojecki concluded that the prevalent mass-mediated Black images of "crime, cheating, violence, low self-discipline" ratify traditional "White fear and rejection" of Blacks and reinforce racial separation.[4] Moreover, Gilens found that such stereotypical images of Blacks inform the white majority's rejection of policies that they wrongly perceive as benefiting mostly African Americans.

While Muslim Americans, Muslims in general, and Islam did not get a great deal of media attention in the past except for the narrow coverage of spectacular episodes, such as terrorist incidents and reactions to those events, the shock of the 9/11 attacks and their grave and long-lasting effects on American policies propelled the Muslim minority in America, Muslims abroad, and their religion higher onto the media agenda and into the public's consciousness. We therefore wondered whether and how the prevalent mass-mediated images of Muslims and Arabs in the entertainment and news media affected the American public's pertinent attitudes and policy preferences.

Less than a year after 9/11, pollsters asked respondents in the United States the following question: Overall, do you think Americans are more likely to feel sympathy for Muslims or are Americans more likely to be fearful of Muslims? Nearly two-thirds (63 percent) of the public thought that Americans were more fearful of Muslims rather than felt sympathy for them; only 12 percent said they were more likely to feel sympathy; 8 percent answered "both," 7 percent said "neither," and 10 percent were not sure. The vast majority of Americans, no doubt, perceived a climate of fear among their fellow citizens with respect to Muslims.[5] Since this particular question was only asked once and did not differentiate between American Muslims and Muslims in general, there was no way to know whether Americans made such a distinction when giving their answers. But one can assume that the predominant mass-mediated images of Muslims as terrorists and as otherwise brutal and violent people that we described in the previous chapters impacted the public's sentiments. This seemed particularly true for the abovementioned fear factor. Indeed, researchers concluded that:

Americans who watched television news more frequently reported higher levels of fear and anxiety after 9/11. These findings raise questions, for example, about the wisdom of replaying coverage of the demise of the World Trade Center towers. Such images are impossible to forget and replaying them may serve to maintain or further amplify fear and anxiety, long after a terrorist incident. The visual imagery of TV seems to be the key to the heightened levels of fear and anxiety among avid media consumers. Reading newspapers increases knowledge levels just as much as television viewing, but has no effect on fear and perception of fear.[6]

Since we know that the overwhelming majority of Americans get most or all of their news from television and not from print, the impact of television images on the public deserves particular attention in the context of terrorism and counterterrorism—especially because it is not short-lived. In fact, more than three years after 9/11, Erik C. Nisbet and James Shanahan found evidence in survey data that "[r]espondents who pay a high level of attention to television news about national politics and the War on Terror are more likely (43 percent vs. 31 percent) to believe that a terrorist attack will occur in the next 12 months than those who pay low attention to television."[7] In the post-9/11 months high fear levels seemed not to intensify public distrust of Arab Americans (and by extension of Muslim Americans since most people believe mistakenly that all or most Arab Americans are also adherents of Islam); instead, survey research established that "fearful and non-fearful respondents held equally negative stereotypes" of this minority.[8] But the fear factor affected how Americans felt about counterterrorist policies. Researchers found more than three years after 9/11 that individuals with a high degree of fear of more terrorist strikes were far more supportive of government measures designed to restrict Muslim Americans' civil liberties than were people with low levels of anxiety and fear.[9]

Following the quadruple bombings of London's transit system on July 7, 2005, many Americans feared similar strikes in the United States. Because the perpetrators of the deadly terrorism in London were identified as homegrown Muslim extremists, there was a mass-mediated debate on the likelihood of terrorist cells in the United States prepared to strike along the lines of the London team. The focus was on Muslims in America as a terrorist threat—although those in charge of additional security measures (for example, in the New York subway and train stations) went out of their way to assure the public that Muslims and Arabs were not the targets of profiling. According to a CBS News poll, 94 percent of the U.S. public believed at the time that terrorists were living in the United States and planning to launch future attacks.[10] Yet, in spite of a heightened terrorism threat alert for the mass transit systems in New York City and elsewhere that the Department of Homeland Security issued and the common association between terrorism and Muslim extremists, opinion polls revealed that the U.S. public's views about Muslim Americans and Islam did not change but were either unchanged or even slightly more favorable than in earlier surveys. Notably, however, one of five Americans claimed, when they were asked about their views about their Muslim compatriots, that they did not know, and one of four gave the same answers with respect to the religion of Islam.[11]

While the polling results seemed indicative of a rational American public that was able to differentiate between a very small number of anti-American and anti-Western Islamist terrorists on the one hand and the religion of Islam, Muslim Americans, and most Muslims abroad, one wonders nevertheless about the large proportion of respondents who claimed to have no opinions on these questions. Asked about this, one expert simply said that "there are still large swaths of people in the country who don't have day-to-day experience with Muslims."[12] But since most survey respondents are generally not deterred by their lack of personal experience and knowledge from expressing explicit opinions on a range of topics and issues, this explanation was not convincing at all. Perhaps "the spiral of silence," which a German expert on survey research once described, was a more plausible explanation for the fact that 25 percent of the public did not reveal an opinion at all and a solid majority described their attitude toward Muslim Americans as positive.[13] The "spiral of silence" concept (or what now is described with the buzzword "political correctness") refers to the tendency of people not to deviate publicly from what they perceive as politically correct—even if they personally think differently. In order to protect what Elisabeth Noelle-Neumann called their "social skin," these people either join the pack in their public utterances—including responses to surveys—or they remain silent.

While nobody knows what percentage of the public succumbs to what they perceive as the climate of opinion at a given time and on a given issue, the "spiral of silence" thesis may explain why the public's expressed overall views on Muslim Americans and Islam were not necessarily compatible with their opinions on more specific issues, problems, and policies that involved Muslim Americans and their religion. For example, at a time when a majority of Americans consistently said that they had a favorable view of Muslim Americans, nearly one of two Americans supported government measures to curb the civil liberties of Muslim citizens.[14]

Thus, just as "white Americans express considerably more enthusiasm for the principle of racial equality than they do for policies that are designed to bring the principles to life,"[15] after 9/11 the American public at large seemed to express more support for the principle of religious tolerance (in this case toward Muslims and Islam) than for its translation into real-life issues. With these observations in mind, we examined relevant survey data on the American public's views on their Muslim fellow citizens, Muslims overseas, the religion of Islam, and politics and policies related to Muslims and their religion.

PUBLIC KNOWLEDGE AND THE SHRINKING OF THE "NO-OPINION/DO-NOT-KNOW" CROWD

When asked about their attitude toward Muslim Americans in early 1994, about a year after the first World Trade Center bombing, which was planned and carried out by "Muslim" terrorists, four of five respondents were unable or unwilling to provide a favorable or unfavorable rating. By early 2001, however, only three of five respondents did not reveal their opinion about Muslim compatriots. During the period in between, Al Qaeda affiliates launched major attacks against American targets abroad (in 1996 on the U.S. military's Khobar Towers housing area in Dharan, Saudi Arabia; in 1998 on the U.S. embassies in Kenya and Tanzania; and in 2000 on the Navy destroyer USS *Cole* in the port of Aden, Yemen) and these events may have affected the American public's opinion about Muslims in their midst or their willingness to reveal their views. Following 9/11, there was yet another decline in the sizable minority of those Americans who couldn't or wouldn't characterize their sentiments in this respect. Finally, after the bombings of the London transit system in early July 2005 by homegrown British Muslims and amid speculations about possible terrorist cells among homegrown Muslims in the United States, only one of five Americans claimed not to know whether they looked upon Muslim Americans in a favorable or unfavorable light.[16] Nevertheless, a strikingly high number of Americans remained who allegedly had no opinions on Muslim fellow citizens.

Similarly, the number of Americans who said they had no opinion about or had not heard enough to render an opinion with respect to Islam was extremely high before 9/11. When surveyed in February 1993, shortly after the first World Trade Center bombing, which was immediately attributed to "Muslim" terrorists, 56 percent of respondents said that they hadn't heard enough to say what they thought of Islam and an additional 8 percent were either not sure or refused to answer. In other words, 64 percent of the public was unable or unwilling to describe their personal views of Islam as favorable or unfavorable. This changed quite dramatically after the events of 9/11 in that by early 2002 only 35 percent of the public had no opinion about Islam. This number dwindled further in the following years so that from late 2002 through the summer of 2005 about one-fourth of the public fell into the no opinion category.[17] Remarkably, by early 2006, only one of ten Americans did not reveal an opinion when asked about their views of Islam.[18]

When the media coverage of Islam on this subject increased markedly in the post-9/11 period, a majority of Americans indicated that they knew more about Islam than before the attacks on New York and Washington. Yet, when they were asked from fall 2001 through July 2005 to rate their knowledge of Islam, very few Americans (4 percent to 6 percent) felt that they had a great deal of understanding of Islam, less than one-third believed they had "some" knowledge, and about two-thirds or more said they did not know very much or nothing at all.[19] One way to figure out whether people know some of the rudimentary terms and their meaning in Islam is, of course, to ask specific questions. Thus, when Americans were asked in 2002 and 2003 how Muslims refer to God (Allah) and to name the Islamic equivalent of the Bible (Koran), better than four in ten respondents knew the correct answer to both questions in 2002 and 2003. By the end of 2004 and the middle of 2005, one-half—and in one poll 54 percent—of the respondents answered both questions correctly—an improvement over the previous years.[20] To be sure, knowing the meaning of Allah and Koran is far from demonstrating a knowledge of Islam—to establish this would require far more specific questions and in-depth interviews. Still, a person's level of knowledge—in this case of Islam—can affect his or her views on related questions, issues or problems. In fact, surveys revealed that respondents who knew most about Islam had a significantly more favorable attitude toward Muslim Americans and Islam (61 percent and 49 percent) than those with little knowledge (47 percent and 24 percent). Similarly, 44 percent of Americans, who were best informed about Islam, said that their own religion had a lot in common with the Muslim religion, but only 12 percent of the least-informed respondents expressed this belief.[21]

BEYOND THE FAVORABLE PUBLIC
EVALUATION OF MUSLIM AMERICANS

In early 1994, when pollsters asked the American public for the first time to reveal their views about Muslim Americans, more respondents (36 percent) expressed unfavorable than favorable views (23 percent). But as table 4.1 shows, beginning in the summer of 2000 and in the immediate aftermath of the terrorist attack against the USS *Cole* about 50 percent of the public described their attitudes toward American Muslims consistently as favorable, with the rest split between those who viewed the Muslim minority unfavorably and those who did not reveal an opinion on this.

But different groups have had quite different attitudes toward Muslim Americans according to racial, ethnic, religious, gender, age, partisan, and ideological cleavages. For example, while the proportion of those who viewed Muslim Americans in a favorable light was about the same among males and females, women were significantly less inclined than men to view this minority unfavorably, and more women than men claimed to have no opinion on this matter. Perhaps because of the presence of Muslims in their communities or their long experience as a minority, Black Americans had a significantly more positive view of Muslim Americans

Table 4.1 The U.S. Public's Views of Muslim Americans

	Favorable	Unfavorable	Don't Know/N.O.
	(%)	(%)	(%)
3/16–3/23, 1994	23	36	41
8/24–9/10, 2000	50	21	29
3/5–3/18, 2001	45	24	31
9/17–9/18, 2001	56	19	26
11/13–11/19, 2001	59	17	24
2/25–3/10, 2002	54	22	24
6/24–7/8, 2003	51	24	25
7/7–7/17, 2005	55	25	20

Sources: Pew Research Center/Pew Forum on Religion and Public Life, Zogby International

than Whites and Latinos did. Adults under fifty years old viewed the Muslim minority far more positively than the fifty-to-sixty-four-year-old group and even more so than seniors sixty-five years and older. College graduates and those with yearly family incomes over $75,000 were far more favorably inclined toward Muslim Americans than were Americans without high school degrees and those with less than $25,000 yearly family income.[22] As for religious affiliations, Black Protestants and White Catholics had far more favorable attitudes toward Muslim Americans than White Protestants. Democrats felt more positive about their Muslim compatriots than Independents and significantly more so than Republicans. Similarly, ideological preferences mattered greatly. For example, a survey in the summer of 2005 revealed that 70 percent of Americans who identified themselves as "liberal Democrats" viewed their Muslim compatriots favorably, whereas 59 percent of conservative and moderate Democrats, 57 percent of moderate and liberal Republicans, and 46 percent of conservative Republicans did. Finally, nearly four years after the attacks on the World Trade Center 50 percent of Americans who approved of Bush's performance in office were favorably inclined toward the Muslim minority, compared to 61 percent of those who did not approve of the president.[23] When Americans were asked more than a year before the 2004 presidential election whether they would vote for "a generally well-qualified person for president who happened to be Muslim" and was nominated by their party, 56 percent said they would cast their ballot for such a candidate, 38 percent said no, and 6 percent did not answer.[24]

But although these survey results showed more favorable than unfavorable views toward Muslim Americans in general, they were often at odds with the public's more specific attitudes about this minority. Shortly after 9/11, for example, when a solid majority of Americans said they had favorable views of Muslim Americans and only two of ten were unfavorably inclined, better than four in ten Americans believed that the terrorist attacks represented "the desires and feelings of Muslim American citizens toward the US" to a large degree (14 percent) or to some degree (30 percent) with an additional 25 percent saying "not very much." This meant that more than two-thirds of the public thought that Muslim Americans sympathized more or less with the motives of the 9/11 terrorists; only one in four respondents felt that Muslim citizens had "not at all" such sentiments.[25] In the spring of 2002, one of five Americans believed that at least half of all Muslim Americans were "anti-American"; another 62 percent thought that "some" or "just a few" were unpatriotic, while 18 percent dodged the question by choosing the "don't know" option.[26] No wonder, then, that more than half a year after 9/11 a sizable plurality of Americans (44 percent) agreed with the suggestion that American Muslims had not done enough to help U.S. authorities to track down terrorist cell members inside the United States, while a large segment of the public (32 percent) claimed not to have an opinion and a smaller minority (24 percent) disagreed with the proposition.[27] Also, at a time when only one in five Americans said that they had an unfavorable opinion of their Muslim compatriots, 44 percent thought that Muslims posed a large (14 percent) or small (30 percent) threat to the "moral character of this country," while another 44 percent did not see such a threat and 12 percent did not answer the question.[28]

INTENSE FEAR OF TERRORISM TRANSLATES INTO PREJUDICE

A vast majority of Americans distinguished between Muslim and Arab citizens and noncitizens when it came to civil liberty issues. When asked whether an Arab or Muslim of foreign nationality should be granted the same legal rights as U.S. citizens when arrested as a suspected terrorist, a solid majority of the public thought that such a person should have fewer rights. When asked the same question with respect to Arab and Muslim citizens, three in five respondents opted for granting them all the rights that any other citizen is entitled to. And yet, one of five respondents was in favor of giving those citizens fewer rights.[29] Indeed, even with more distance from the 9/11 events, a sizable minority of Americans favored restricting the civil liberties of all Muslim Americans—not just of those who were suspected terrorists and put behind bars. This was the troublesome result of a survey conducted by the Media and Research Group at Cornell University in the fall of 2004. Respondents were asked the following specific questions:

- Should Muslim Americans be required to register their whereabouts with the federal government?
- Should mosques be closely monitored and surveyed by U.S. enforcement agencies?

- Should law enforcement agencies profile citizens as potential threats based on being Muslim or having Middle Eastern heritage?
- Should Muslim civic and volunteer organizations be infiltrated by undercover law enforcement agents to keep watch on their activities and fundraising?

Twenty-nine percent of the respondents were in favor of infiltrating Muslim organizations, 27 percent agreed with the proposition that all Muslim Americans should register their whereabouts with the government, 26 percent were for the surveillance of mosques, and 22 percent supported the profiling of Muslims and those of Middle Eastern background. While 48 percent were not in favor of any of the above measures, 44 percent supported at least one, with 8 percent in the "don't know/refuse-to-answer" category.[30] There were, however, significant differences in the positions based on respondents' fear of terrorism, party affiliation, religious fervor, and consumption of television news. The responses to all four questions showed that Republicans were in each case far more supportive of restricting American Muslims' civil liberties than Democrats and Independents. For example, while 40 percent of Republicans favored the proposition that Muslim compatriots should be forced to register their whereabouts, only 24 percent of Democrats and 17 percent of Independents supported such a measure. Similarly, 34 percent of Republicans were for profiling Muslim citizens compared to only 17 percent of Democrats and 15 percent of Independents.

Individuals who revealed a high degree of fear of terrorist strikes were much more inclined to support curbs on Muslim Americans' civil liberties on all four counts than were their less fearful brethren. For example, whereas 41 percent of the highly fearful respondents favored the infiltration of Muslim American civic organizations, only 21 percent of those with low-level fears of terrorism supported this proposition. Also, highly religious Americans proved to be far more in favor of all four civil liberties restrictions for Muslim citizens than respondents with moderate and low levels of religiosity. Thus, 42 percent of highly religious respondents favored requiring Muslims to register their whereabouts with government compared to 30 percent of those with moderate and 15 percent of those with low religiosity.[31]

AMERICAN MUSLIMS: CIVIC AND PUBLIC LIFE AND EXERCISE OF THEIR RELIGION

Discriminatory sentiments with respect to Muslim Americans' religious organizations and participation in social services and religious practices preceded the events of 9/11 but increased thereafter. When pollsters asked in March 2001 what religious groups should be allowed to apply for government funds to support their social services, a clear majority of respondents were in favor of Catholic, Protestant, and evangelical Christian churches, synagogues, and the Mormon Church, but a plurality (46 percent) did not want Muslim mosques to compete for such funds.[32] However, a month earlier when reminded that the newly elected President George W. Bush encouraged the funding of religious organizations so that they could provide social services, 62 percent of respondents had approved of Muslim organizations' participation in such a program.[33] But after the attacks on New York and Washington there were frequent news reports about alleged contributions to terrorist groups by American Muslim organizations, among them religious ones, and Bush administration measures to shut down such funding sources. Not surprisingly therefore, three months after 9/11 four of five Americans felt that President Bush did the right thing in freezing the assets of Islamic religious charities. Moreover, it seemed that in the minds of many non-Muslim Americans, all Muslim organizations were suspect. Thus, two years after 9/11, when pollsters inquired whether social programs like day-care and drug rehabilitation programs run by Islamic organizations should receive federal funds, a clear majority (57 percent) of the public said no.[34] These negative attitudes hardened the public's sentiments about American Muslims' exercise of their religion. In March 1993, when asked whether American Muslims should be allowed days off with pay to observe major Muslim holidays, a plurality (49 percent) was against the proposition. But at the same time, public opinion was split between those who were for and against the suggestion that school cafeterias should recognize the dietary needs of Muslim students.[35] Nearly a decade later, in July 2004, public opinion seemed more solidly opposed to accommodating the religious customs of their Muslim compatriots in that 57 percent felt that employers should not be required to allow deeply religious Muslim workers to take two or three breaks each day for religious observances.[36]

LESS PUBLIC SYMPATHY FOR
ISLAM THAN FOR MUSLIM AMERICANS

When asked in the wake of the first World Trade Center bombing in February 1993 about their views of Islam, a solid majority of respondents (56 percent) chose the "haven't heard enough to say" option and an additional 8 percent picked "not sure" or refused to answer. Of the remaining respondents, slightly more than one-third of those in the respondent pool, 22 percent saw Islam in an unfavorable light while 14 percent were favorably inclined.[37] When given the "haven't heard enough to say" option during the year following the 9/11 attacks, respondents continued to express more unfavorable than favorable views. Yet, as table 4.2 shows, when pollsters asked the same question without explicitly listing the "haven't heard enough to say" choice, the results changed. From early 2002 on, the public expressed more positive than negative attitudes toward Islam—although the differences between the two sides were often within the margins of error range and pointed to a fairly evenly divided situation among those who were able or willing to express an opinion. In early 2006, for the first time there were significantly more respondents revealing an unfavorable view of Islam than those expressing a favorable attitude.[38] In the days after 9/11 more Americans than not believed that the attacks represented to one degree or the other the true teachings of Islam. Nearly a year later, the public was evenly split on this question.[39]

But this much was clear: Throughout the post-9/11 years, the American public had a more positive opinion of Muslim Americans than of the religion of Islam.

Just as different demographic groups had vastly different attitudes toward Muslim Americans, the same cleavages existed with respect to public opinion on Islam. Blacks viewed Islam far more positively than other racial groups; Whites were evenly divided between those who saw Islam in a positive and a negative light; and Latinos were far more unsympathetic toward the Muslim religion than sympathetic. People under fifty years of age had more favorable views of Islam than the older generations. Males were far more forthcoming in expressing their views on Islam than females, but

Table 4.2.   U.S. Public Opinion on Islam (With "Haven't Heard Enough to Say" Option)

	Haven't heard enough to say	Favorable	Unfavorable	Not sure/ refused answer
	(%)	(%)	(%)	(%)
2/18–2/19, 1993	56	14	22	8
2/24–2/26, 2002	31	30	33	6
8/22–2/25, 2002	26	26	38	9
2/22–2/26, 2006	32	23	36	9

U.S. Public Opinion on Islam (Without "Haven't Heard Enough to Say" Option)

	Favorable	Unfavorable	No Opinion
	(%)	(%)	(%)
1/2–1/6, 2002	41	24	35
2/24–3/10, 2002	38	33	29
10/11–10/15, 2002	42	33	26
6/24–7/8, 2003	40	34	26
9/4–9/7, 2003	39	38	23
7/8–7/18, 2004	39	37	24
7/7–7/17, 2005	39	36	25
3/2–3/5, 2006	43	46	11

Sources: Los Angeles Times, CBS News, ABC News/*Washington Post,* and Pew Research Center for the People and the Press

there was no significant gender difference with respect to favorable versus unfavorable evaluations of Islam by men and women. A very solid majority of college graduates were sympathetic toward Islam as were a clear plurality of people with some college education, whereas a large plurality of high school graduates and an even larger plurality of those without high school degrees revealed unfavorable views of Islam. Americans with high incomes were far more likely to express favorable attitudes toward Islam than were persons with lesser family incomes and especially those in the lowest income bracket.

Americans in the East and to a lesser extent in the West were in larger numbers sympathetic toward the Muslim religion than their compatriots in the Midwest and South. Black Protestants followed by White Catholics, Non-Evangelical White Protestants, and secular Americans were far more positive than negative in their assessment of Islam while Evangelical White Protestants saw Islam overwhelmingly in a negative light. As for party affiliation, solid pluralities of Republicans and of those who approved of President George W. Bush's job performance had unfavorable views of Islam, contrary to clear pluralities among Democrats and Independents who saw the Muslim religion in a positive light.[40]

ISLAM—DIFFERENT FROM OTHER RELIGIONS?

Following the events of 9/11 pollsters asked all kinds of questions about Islam designed to establish whether Americans considered the Muslim religion to be very different from Christianity, Judaism, Buddhism, and so on, and, just as important, whether the U.S. public associated the 9/11 type of violence with Islamic teachings. On the first count, in the years following the attacks in New York and Washington, a majority of the public (52 percent in 2001, 57 percent in 2002, 60 percent in 2003, and 59 percent in 2005) considered the religion that Muslims adhere to as "very different" from their own, while less than one-third (31 percent in 2001, 27 percent in 2002, 22 percent in 2003, and 27 percent in 2005) felt that their own religion and Islam "have a lot in common."[41] White Catholics, Black Protestants, and White Mainline Protestants were far more likely to find common ground than White Evangelicals.[42] With the identities of the architects and perpetrators of 9/11 fresh in mind, a plurality of Americans (41 percent in January 2002 and 37 percent in October 2002) believed that mainstream Islam does not teach respect for the beliefs of non-Muslims, but by September 2003 public opinion had flip-flopped in that a 43 percent plurality believed mainstream Islam to preach tolerance vis-à-vis other religions. While one wonders what to make of these poll results in view of the large number of respondents (28 percent to 38 percent) who claimed to have no opinion,[43] other surveys with less general question wordings were helpful in solving this puzzle. For example, when pollsters brought up Islam's and Muslims' tolerance in a very different context, the respondents were far more willing to express opinions and thereby were far more likely to evaluate Islam and Muslims as intolerant. For example, in June 2005 the following question was asked of respondents: "At the prison at Guantanamo Bay, Muslim prisoners are given copies of the holy Muslim book the Koran. If Muslims were holding Americans as prisoners, do you think the Americans would be given copies of the Bible?" 75 percent said "no," only 10 percent "yes," and 10 percent said they were not sure or refused to answer.[44]

On the second count, when first asked in early 2002 whether Islam is more likely than other religions to encourage violence among its believers, Americans seemed to be still influenced by President George W. Bush's post-9/11 appeals for tolerance toward Muslims and Islam. Thus, two of four respondents told pollsters that in their mind Islam was not different in this respect than other religions, and only one in four thought of the Muslim religion as encouraging violence or did not voice an opinion. But when the president and other leaders did not renew their calls for tolerance while religious leaders condemned Islam as violent and evil, the public sentiment vis-à-vis Islam changed drastically. As table 4.3 demonstrates, in 2003 and 2004 more Americans considered Islam more likely to encourage violence than other religions before the pendulum swung back in 2005—albeit not to the levels of early 2002. But when asked in early 2006 whether, in comparison to other religions, "there are more violent extremists within Islam, fewer, or about the same number," a clear majority (58 percent) of Americans chose the "more" option and one-third said the number was about the same as in other religions.[45] It is conceivable that the daily coverage of violence in Iraq contributed to this opinion shift.

Gender, race, age, religious affiliation, party identification, ideological preferences, and individual approval or disapproval of the president affected Americans' attitudes in this respect, whereas educational and family income

Table 4.3. Is Islam More Likely Than Other Religions to Encourage Violence among Its Believers?

	More likely to encourage violence	Not more likely to encourage violence	Neither/Don't know
	(%)	(%)	(%)
2/25–3/10, 2002	25	51	24
6/24–7/8, 2003	44	41	15
7/8–7/18, 2004	46	37	17
7/7–7/17, 2005	36	47	17

Source: The Pew Research Center for the People and the Press

levels did not. Women were less inclined than men to classify Islam as more in favor of violence than other religions. The under-thirty-year-olds more than the older generations recognized the same traits in all religions, while Whites and Hispanics emphasized the violent nature of Islam far more than their Black compatriots. The contrast between Americans who approved of President Bush's job performance and those who disapproved was especially pronounced in that significantly more Bush supporters (48 percent in 2003 and 44 percent in 2005) than his critics (38 percent in 2003 and 30 percent in 2005) looked upon Islam as more violent than other religions. Republicans far more than Democrats or Liberals and White Protestants significantly more than White Catholics, Black Protestants, and Seculars thought Islam to be more likely to encourage violence than other religions.[46]

But as researchers at Cornell University found, the intensity of religious devotion more than mere religious affiliation had the strongest effects on how non-Muslim Americans considered Islam's and other religions' propensity for violence. While 65 percent of those individuals who identified themselves as highly religious considered Islam more violent than other religions, 54 percent of the moderately religious identifiers and only 42 percent of those with a low level of religiosity did so.[47]

Finally, the answers to follow-up questions reveal at times that initial responses should be taken with a grain of salt and scrutinized, as explained earlier, in the context of the spiral of silence or political correctness context. For example, when respondents who said that Islam didn't encourage violence more than other religions were subsequently asked whether they considered Christianity, Islam, Judaism, or Hinduism as most violent, 60 percent picked Islam, and 11 percent Christianity before Judaism and Hinduism with 4 percent each.[48]

ISLAMIC FUNDAMENTALISM SEEN AS SERIOUS THREAT

Questions about the growth of "Islamic fundamentalism" as a threat to American security and interest were first raised in the late 1980s—well before the events of 9/11. Thus, as early as 1988 a large plurality of the public felt that this was an "extremely serious" threat (17 percent) or a "very serious threat" (28 percent) while 14 percent thought the danger was "not important" and 14 percent were not sure. In the fall of 1994, when the first World Trade Center bombing was still fresh in their minds, 69 percent of Americans considered the possible expansion of Islamic fundamentalism as a "critical" (33 percent) or "important but not critical" (36 percent) threat to the vital interest of the United States in the next ten years.[49]

After 9/11, when asked whether terrorist attacks by Islamists "are part of a major conflict between the people of America and Europe versus the people of Islam" or whether this is a conflict with "a small, radical group," a majority (63 percent in late 2001, 52 percent in August 2002, and 60 percent in July 2005) of the public picked the small-group option while a minority (28 percent in 2001, 35 percent in 2002, and 29 percent in 2005) opted for the "clash of civilizations" scenario à la Samuel Huntington.[50] But even many of those respondents who thought in terms of a confrontation with a small number of extremists at the time expected nevertheless that this problem would grow "into a major world conflict."[51] This, then, was again a case in which the reply to a follow-up inquiry revealed assessments and sentiments that were not at all revealed by the initial answers.

Moreover, different question wordings produced different answers. When respondents to a survey commissioned by Fox News were asked pointedly whether they agreed or disagreed that "the threat of radical Islamic terrorism today is similar to the threat posed by war with communism in the last century," 48 percent replied with yes, 38 percent with no, and 14 percent said they did not know. When asked to evaluate the "threat of Islamic fundamentalism to the United States in the next 10 years," a vast majority of Americans (83 percent in 2003, 87 percent in 2004, and 79 percent in 2005) chose the "extremely important" or "important" options.[52] Similar surveys produced similar results in that this threat was perceived as critical or at least important by around 80 percent of the respondents. Moreover, one of two Americans felt it was very or somewhat likely that he or she would be personally affected by "the more radical stream of Islam."[53]

THE U.S. PUBLIC AND MUSLIMS IN GENERAL

Just as after 9/11 the U.S. public expressed consistently more favorable than unfavorable views of American Muslims in public opinion surveys, rank-and-file Americans also expressed far more positive than negative views when asked directly about their sentiments toward Muslims in general.[54] But during that same time period nearly two-thirds of Americans (71 percent) thought that the "Muslim world considered itself at war with the United States," while two-thirds believed as well that the United States was not at war with the Muslim world.[55] Similarly, a year after the 9/11 attacks over half of the public (56 percent) believed that Muslims abroad sympathized with those who destroyed the World Trade Center and part of the Pentagon; only 11 percent thought that Muslims in other countries sided with the United States.[56] Consistent with these views of Muslims abroad, three in four or better than four in five Americans were in favor of tightening immigration laws in order to restrict the number of immigrants from

Arab and Muslim countries to the United States.[57] There was even suspicion concerning legal immigrants from Arab and Muslim countries already inside the country: better than half of the public strongly favored that the whereabouts of these people be closely monitored by the authorities and another 29 percent accepted such a solution; only 25 percent opposed such a measure as going too far.[58]

When pollsters asked Americans nearly a year after 9/11 to "rate their feelings toward some countries and peoples, with one hundred meaning a very warm, favorable feeling, zero meaning a very cold, unfavorable feeling, and fifty meaning not particularly warm or cold," 36 percent of respondents rated their sentiments toward "The Muslim people" as being in the warm range, 32 percent in the cold range, and 25 percent at the neutral point. But two years later, in 2004, the American public's feelings toward "the Muslim people" had changed in that 44 percent rated their sentiments in the cold range and only 22 percent in the warm range, while 22 percent picked the neutral point. In other words, while the American public's feelings toward Muslims in general were lukewarm in the summer of 2002, by 2004 they had cooled off in a dramatic fashion.[59]

CONCLUSION: AMERICA'S UNEASY VIEW OF MUSLIMS AND ISLAM

A majority of Americans gave mostly politically correct answers when asked to answer standard questions giving negative versus positive options concerning Muslim Americans, Islam, and Muslims abroad; but in response to more specific inquiries, the majority or at least a sizable plurality of the public revealed less sympathetic and indeed prejudicial attitudes toward Muslims and their religion. While Americans held on to an embrace of religious freedom and religious practices for Muslims in America as manifested, for example, by the majority's support for allowing Muslim females to wear their head scarves in schools, places of business, and elsewhere in public, the experiences of 9/11 and of subsequent major terrorist attacks abroad raised Americans' uneasy feelings about people in Muslim countries and their religion. It seems that these sentiments spilled over into non-Muslim Americans' attitudes toward Muslim citizens in their midst. Indeed, when everything was said and done, many Americans seemed to attribute some responsibility for terrorist acts by a small number of non-American Islamists to all of their Muslim compatriots. That is the only plausible explanation why a majority of Americans believed that "people of the Muslim faith in the United States have a special obligation to help authorities to track down terrorists and defeat Osama bin Laden."[60]

NOTES

1. Martin Gilens, *Why Americans Hate Welfare: Race, Media, and the Politics of Antipoverty Policy* (Chicago: University of Chicago Press, 1999), chapter 6.

2. Walter Lippmann, *Public Opinion* (1922; repr. New York: The Free Press, 1997), 229.

3. Robert M. Entman and Andrew Rojecki, *The Black Image in the White Mind* (Chicago: University of Chicago Press, 2000).

4. Entman and Rojecki, *Black Image*, chapter 12.

5. The survey was conducted by Opinion Dynamics for Fox News on June 18–19, 2002.

6. Leonie Huddy et al., "Fear and Terrorism: Psychological Reactions to 9/11," in Pippa Norris, Montague Kern, and Marion Just, *Framing Terrorism: The News Media, the Government, and the Public* (New York: Routledge, 2003), 273

7. Erik C. Nisbet and James Shanahan, "MSRG Special Report: Restrictions on Civil Liberties, Views of Islam, & Muslim Americans," Media and Society Group, Cornell University, December 2005, 2.

8. Huddy et al., "Fear and Terrorism." 269.

9. Nisbet and Shanahan, "MSRG Special Report," 6.

10. The CBS News survey was conducted July 13–14, 2005. Only 3 percent of the respondents said there were no terrorists inside the United States planning terrorist attacks; 3 percent did not know or had no opinion.

11. According to polls conducted by the Pew Research Center for the People and the Press/Pew Forum on Religion and Public Life and ABC News.

12. Rita Ciolli, "Poll: Views of Muslims same despite bombs," *Newsday*, July 27, 2005, A25.

13. Elisabeth Noelle-Neumann, *The Spiral of Silence: Public Opinion—Our Social Skin.* (Chicago: University of Chicago Press, 1984).

14. According to the 2004 national omnibus survey of public opinion and media use, conducted between October 25 and November 23, 2004, by the Media and Society Research Group at Cornell University, Ithaca, New York, in cooperation with the ILR Survey Research Institute.

15. Donald R. Kinder and Lynn M. Sanders, *Divided by Color: Racial Politics and Democratic Ideals* (Chicago: University of Chicago Press, 1996), 6.

16. According to eight surveys conducted from March 1994 to July 2005 by the Pew Research Center/Pew Forum on Religion and Public Life and Zogby International.

17. According to opinion surveys conducted by the *Los Angeles Times*, CBS News, ABC News, and the Pew Research Center for the People and the Press.

18. According to an ABC News/*Washington Post* survey conducted March 2–5, 2006 and a CBS News poll conducted February 22–26, 2006.

19. According to four surveys conducted in November 2001, March 2002, July 2003, and July 2005 by the Pew Research Center for the People and the Press and four ABC News polls conducted in October 2001, January 2002, October 2002, and September 2003.

20. According to surveys conducted by the Pew Research Center for the People and the Press and by the Media and Society Group at Cornell University.

21. The Pew Research Center for the People and the Press, "Views of Muslim-Americans Hold Steady After London Bombing," survey conducted July 7–17, 2005.

22. The Pew Research Center for the People and the Press, "Views of Islam and Religion in the World," survey conducted February 25–March 10, 2002, and "Views of Muslim-Americans Hold Steady After London Bombing," survey conducted July 7–17, 2005.

23. The Pew Research Center for the People and the Press, "Views of Muslim-Americans Hold Steady After London Bombing," survey conducted July 7–17, 2005.

24. Pew Research Center, Pew Forum on Religion and Public Life, survey conducted June 24–July 8, 2003, by Princeton Survey Research Associates.

25. Wirthlin Worldwide, survey conducted September 15–17, 2001.

26. The Pew Research Center for the People and the Press, "Views of Islam and Religion in the World," survey conducted February 25–March 10, 2002.

27. Fox News/Opinion Dynamics, survey conducted April 2–3, 2002.

28. Institute for Jewish and Community Research, survey conducted May 3–7, 2002.

29. National Public Radio/Henry Kaiser Foundation, Harvard University Kennedy School of Government, survey conducted August 7–11, 2002.

30. The comprehensive national omnibus survey was conducted by the Media and Society Research Group at Cornell University, October 25–November 23, 2004.

31. Media and Society Research Group, survey conducted October 25–November 23, 2004.

32. Pew Research Center for the People and the Press, survey conducted March 5–18, 2001.

33. Gallup Organization, poll conducted February 1–4, 2004.

34. Gallup Organization, poll conducted September 19, 2003.

35. American Muslim Council/Zogby Group International, survey conducted March 16–23, 1993.

36. Public Agenda Foundation, survey conducted July 2004.

37. *Los Angeles Times,* poll conducted February 18–19, 2003.

38. According to a CBS News poll conducted February 22–26, 2006.

39. According to a Wirthlin Quorum Poll, conducted September 15–17, 2001, and a survey conducted by the Chicago Council on Foreign Relations on June 1–30, 2002.

40. For attitudes on Islam held by various societal groups, see the survey reports of the Pew Research Center for the People and the Press, February 25–March 10, 2002, and July 7–17, 2005; and that of CBS News, February 22–26, 2002.

41. Pew Research Center for the People and the Press, surveys conducted February 25–March 10, 2002, and July 7–17, 2005; and CBS News, survey conducted February 22–26, 2002.

42. Pew Research Center for the People and the Press, surveys conducted February 25–March 10, 2002, and July 7–17, 2005; and CBS News, survey conducted February 22–26, 2002.

43. ABC News polls, conducted January 2–6, 2002; October 11–14, 2002; and September 4–7, 2003.

44. Fox News/Opinion Dynamics Poll, conducted June 14–15, 2005.

45. ABC News/*Washington Post,* survey conducted March 2–5, 2006.

46. The Pew Research Center for the People and the Press, surveys conducted by Princeton Survey Research Associates, February 25–March 10, 2002; June 24–July 8, 2003; and July 7–17, 2005.

47. Nisbet and Shanahan, "MSRG Special Report," 5.

48. The Pew Research Center for the People and the Press, survey conducted July 7–17, 2005.

49. Survey by Americans Talk Security, conducted by Daniel Yankelovich Group, September 30–October 4, 1988; Survey by Chicago Council on Foreign Relations, conducted by Gallup Organization, October 7–25, 1995.

50. Pew Research Center Surveys, conducted by Princeton Survey Research Associates, October 15–21, 2001; August 14–24, 2002; and July 7–17, 2005.

51. Pew Research Center for the People and the Press, "Views of Muslim-Americans hold steady after London bombings," survey conducted July 26, 2005.

52. Transatlantic Trends 2003/2004/2005 Surveys conducted by the German Marshall Fund of the United States, Compagnia di San Paolo.

53. Transatlantic Trends 2005 Survey conducted by the German Marshall Fund of the United States, Compagnia di San Paolo.

54. According to Zogby International, Gallup, and the Pew Research Center for the People and the Press the favorable versus unfavorable ratio with respect to Muslims in general was 44–29 in September 2001, 66–27 in November 2001, and 48–32 in February 2004.

55. Gallup/CNN/*USA Today*, poll conducted March 1–3, 2002.

56. Institute for Social Research at the University of North Carolina, survey conducted August 26–September 3, 2002.

57. Wirthlin Quorum Poll, conducted September 15–17, 2001, and Chicago Council on Foreign Relations/German Marshall Fund, survey conducted June 1–30, 2002.

28. According to *Newsweek*/Princeton Survey Research Associates, survey conducted September 20–21, 2001.

59. According to surveys conducted for the Chicago Council on Foreign Relations in June 2002 and July 2004.

60. Fox News/Opinion Dynamics, polls conducted October 1, 2001, and November 1, 2001.

5

Torture: When the Enemy Fits Prevalent Stereotypes

In March 2002, Ted Koppel of *Nightline* showed participants of an electronic town hall meeting on torture and other civil liberty issues a clip from the long-running hit series *NYPD Blue* in which detective Andy Sipowicz brutally "tuned up" a suspect.[1] A year later, a broadcast of *World News Tonight with Peter Jennings* opened a segment on "torture or persuasion" by showing a torture scene from the motion picture *The Siege* with Bruce Willis. In her voice-over Jackie Judd said, "Hollywood's version of torture knows no limits."[2] As Mark Mcguire, the TV/radio writer of the *Times Union* in Albany, New York, observed in early 2003, "Today on TV, sanctioned torture and murder are condoned like never before, not only by the individual characters, but also their employers."[3] This protorture trend in the entertainment offerings was thought to bolster the support for tough antiterrorism measures that included curbs on civil liberties and human rights values in the name of greater security. According to Robert Thompson, an expert on popular television, "[t]he federal government could not have come up with a better set of [TV] series to prepare its audience for the new order of the day."[4]

The popular television series *24* that featured counterterrorism was a case in point. Take an episode in which Islamic terrorists, coming from a Turkish family living in California, attack a nuclear power plant in the United States. What kind of audience impact does a script have, even when fictitious, that places some of the most ruthless terrorists—Muslims—right into the viewers' own neighborhoods?

In late spring 2005, the former executive editor of the *New York Times*, Joseph Lelyveld, expressed what seemed indicative of most of the U.S. news media's treatment of torture in the post-9/11 climate, when he wrote about

75

the uncertainty of where "to draw the line on the use of coercive force" in the interrogation of terrorists and suspected terrorists. In Lelyveld's words,

> As matters stand, that's up to an administration that after the Sept. 11 attacks entertained an argument that any attempt to enforce the United Nations Convention Against Torture (ratified by the United States, with reservations, in 1994) would be an unconstitutional interference with the powers of the commander-in-chief; an administration that says it abhors torture but prefers not to be pinned down on what it now considers torture to be. That's an issue, we're led to understand, for private negotiations between the C.I.A. and the attorney general. The rest of us can be forgiven if we draw the implication that we're expected to butt out if we can't accept at face value the pious promises of humane treatment for detainees that are regularly served up by administration spokesmen. Instead of worrying about what's real but unknowable, we get to watch the Fox TV counterterrorism serial "24," in which torture is just another tool the good guys have to wield and clean-cut technicians are always on call to administer electric shocks to recalcitrant conspirators.[5]

By pointing to the administration's virtually unquestioned post-9/11 decision-making power and to American TV audiences' familiarity with torturing "bad guys," Lelyveld provided a plausible explanation for the failure of antitorture voices to get traction in the mass media and in the general public—even after the Abu Ghraib horror visuals. After all, research has established that over time heavy television viewers are affected by the predominant values expressed in the programs they watch and that entertainment's influence in this respect does not at all take a backseat to the effects of news programs.[6] This effect, then, may help to explain the absence of massive and sustained outrage and protest when one or the other form of torture was suggested to force terrorists and suspected terrorists to reveal information or when the Abu Ghraib torture scandal broke.

While not at all discounting the influence of the entertainment media, this chapter examines how the news media reported on and framed the issues surrounding the use of torture in the months and years after 9/11. We distinguish between two time periods here: the first beginning with the attacks on New York, the second starting with the first news reports about the torture of inmates by U.S. personnel at the Abu Ghraib prison in Iraq and the publicizing of very graphic visuals. The seemingly hypothetical mass-mediated discourse on torture as a means to extract information from known or suspected terrorists in period I, which moved into the realm of reality following the Abu Ghraib revelations (period II), concerned mostly, if not exclusively, Christians and Westerners physically and psychologically mistreating Muslims and Arabs. Religious, racial, and cultural prejudices clearly figured into the post-9/11 mass-mediated debate on America's enemies in the war on terrorism in general and the pros and cons of torture in particular. Both of these situations were likely to influence the sentiments of the American public, especially Muslim and Arab Americans, and of hundreds of millions in the Muslim world.

FROM 9/11 TO THE ABU GHRAIB PICTURES OF HORROR

In the months following 9/11, the Bush administration and especially Attorney General John Ashcroft pushed the USA PATRIOT Act so rapidly through Congress that most, if not all, members cast their votes before they had an opportunity to fully study the details contained in the bill. In the absence of a compelling story line, sound bites, and visuals, the news media paid little attention to the proposed counterterrorism measures that aimed at preventing further strikes inside the United States. What little was reported focused mostly on the strategies deployed by supporters and opponents of the bill and on speculations about how quickly President George W. Bush would be able to sign the legislation into law. Television news programs in particular did not discharge their responsibility to inform the public about the substance of the massive antiterrorism package and to provide a stage for public debate. While debating the pros and cons of torture in the "war on terrorism" was not particularly high on the news media's agenda either in the months and years after 9/11, the issue was not ignored. Yet, the media's treatment of the torture issue was as unsatisfactory as their shallow reporting on the substance of the Patriot Act. Typically, political talk show hosts, expert guests, reporters, commentators, and columnists handled this subject in a rather cavalier fashion. Even when they mentioned that torture violates international conventions and American values, the loudest and most prominent voices in the media seemed to embrace the view that extraordinary times justify exceptions to the rule.

A case in point was Stuart Taylor Jr., who wrote in the *National Journal*:

> Unlike the 1949 Geneva Convention regarding prisoners of war, the torture convention protects even terrorists and other "unlawful combatants." But its definition of torture—intentional infliction of "severe pain or suffering, whether physical or mental"—leaves room for interpretation. It's a good bet that Khalid Shaikh Mohammed [captured Al Qaeda chief of operations in U.S. custody] has felt some pain. And if that's the best chance of making him talk, it's OK by me.[7]

In his column in *Newsweek*, Jonathan Alter suggested a double standard with respect to rejecting torture—a tough one for the rest of the world and a more lenient one for the United States. Thus, Alter wrote,

> even as we continue to speak out against human-rights violations around the world, we need to keep an open mind about certain measures to fight terrorism,

like court-sanctioned psychological interrogation. And we'll have to think about transferring some suspects to our less squeamish allies, even if that's hypocritical. Nobody said this was going to be pretty.[8]

In a lengthy story in the *Atlantic Monthly*, Mark Bowden distinguished between hard-core torture and torture lite, or what he suggested should be called "coercion." With respect to torture lite, Bowden wrote, "Although excruciating for the victim, these tactics leave no permanent marks and do no lasting physical harm."[9] In the closing paragraphs of his article Bowden embraced torture lite (which according to his description seemed far from lite) and recommended a curious double standard:

> The Bush Administration has adopted exactly the right posture on the matter. Candor and consistency are not always public virtues. Torture is a crime against humanity, but coercion is an issue that is rightly handled with a wink, or even a touch of hypocrisy; it should be banned but also quietly practiced.
>
> It is wise of the President to reiterate U.S. support for international agreements banning torture, and it is wise for American interrogators to employ whatever coercive methods work. It is also smart not to discuss the matter with anyone.
>
> If interrogators step over the line from coercion to outright torture, they should be held personally responsible. But no interrogator is ever going to be prosecuted for keeping Khalid Sheikh Mohammed awake, cold, alone, and uncomfortable. Nor should he be.[10]

In other words, do it but do not admit it and do not get caught.

After his article was published, Bowden was interviewed on several TV programs. The hosts and anchors seemed not at all uncomfortable with his views. At the end of Bowden's appearance on NBC's *Today Show*, for example, co-anchor Matt Lauer seemed at ease with his guest's do-it-but-do-not-tell position. He even adopted his guest's preference for the term "coercion," as the following exchange illustrated:

> *Lauer:* In 10 seconds left, we're on a slippery slope. If the government agrees to coercion on rare occasions because national security or—or human safety is at risk, what is the risk of them allowing it all the time?
>
> *Bowden:* Well, it is a real problem and it actually happened in Israel. And I think the answer is to be somewhat hypocritical, to ban it but to practice it, basically, so that the person, the interrogator, takes upon himself or herself the responsibility and potentially can be prosecuted for using these techniques. And that's [*sic*] acts as sort of a self-limiting factor.
>
> *Lauer:* Mark Bowden, Mark, always good to have you here.

It was a rather nonchalant end to a pleasant conversation about an awfully troubling issue.

On the television networks, experts in favor of torture were represented more frequently than were critics of this extreme interrogation method. When opponents of torture did appear on such shows, they were typically drawn from human rights and civil liberties organizations and allotted less time to articulate their arguments than were the supporters of any form or some type of torture.

In his book *Why Terrorism Works*, Harvard Law Professor Alan Dershowitz does not argue in favor of wholesale torture but suggests legalizing torture in extreme cases when a judge can be convinced of a "ticking bomb" scenario in which a detainee is believed to have knowledge of an imminent terrorist act and torture is seen as the only chance to get the information that would prevent the terrorist strike. Professor Dershowitz published op-ed pieces that explained his view on limited legalized torture and was repeatedly interviewed on high-profile TV network programs—twice on CBS, three times on NBC. The search words "Alan Dershowitz" and "torture" materialized several dozen hits in the LexisNexis all-transcripts category for the two-year period from October 1, 2001 to September 30, 2003.

In his book *Terrorism, Freedom, and Security: Winning without War*, Harvard Law Professor and former deputy attorney general of the United States Philip Heymann rejects torture categorically, regardless of whether the method is used by U.S. interrogators or by foreign proxies. As for the legalized torture á la Dershowitz, Heyman warns that the use of torture would drastically increase if there were torture warrants as suggested by his colleague. According to Heymann, "Judges have deferred to the last fourteen thousand requests for national security wiretaps and they would defer here."[11] While Dershowitz received ample opportunity to explain his conditional protorture stand in the media, his Harvard colleague's opposition to torture did not—with one exception: on February 16, 2002, the *Boston Globe* ran opinion pieces by Dershowitz and Heymann side by side on the same op-ed page. But neither Heymann nor other experts with similar views received the TV exposure of Dershowitz and other proponents of limited or all-out torture.

Given this guest and source selection, there were comparably few voices in the news that categorically condemned torture whether by Americans or by proxy. One of the exceptions was Jonathan Turley, who wrote in his op-ed piece in the *Los Angeles Times*,

This week, West Virginia Sen. John D. Rockefeller actually encouraged the U.S. to hand over the recently arrested Al Qaeda suspect Khalid Shaikh Mohammed to another country for torture. Whatever legal distinction Rockefeller sees in using surrogates to do our torturing, it is hardly a moral distinction. As a result, we are now driving the new market for torture-derived information. We have gone from a nation that once condemned torture to one that contracts out for torture services.[12]

In the *Washington Post* Richard Cohen expressed surprise that there had not been a public reaction after the *Post*'s disclosure that the Bush administration had shipped some suspected terrorists to foreign countries notorious for torturing prisoners during interrogations. But Cohen did not unequivocally oppose the torturing of terrorists either. Instead, he wrote,

> When it comes to torture—especially its more benign variations (sleep deprivation, shaking, etc.)—I would never say never. But those who counsel us to "get real" have a heavy obligation to confront a different kind of reality. Torture is a beast with a rapacious appetite. The French wound up using it indiscriminately in Algeria; the Argentine junta, faced with a terrorist threat as real as our own, also tortured on a grand scale.
>
> Civilization is threatened not only by terrorists but also by the means we use to fight them.[13]

Some of the leading newspapers took clear editorial stands against the United States using torture in the fight against terrorism. The *Washington Post*, for example, published two such editorials in the two years after 9/11. In the late 2002, the *Post* stated in an editorial that "there are certain things democracies don't do, even under duress, and torture is high on the list."[14] Nearly three months later, when protorture voices exploited the arrest of Al Qaeda's chief of operations Khalid Sheikh Mohammed, the same editorial page reminded readers, "the United States has signed international treaties forbidding torture, and forswearing such brutality is a fundamental commitment of civilized government as exists. It is incumbent on the administration to clarify that the war on terrorism is not including barbarism of its own."[15] A number of other newspapers across the country also editorialized against allowing torture at home or abroad. Others rejected torture most of the time but accepted it in the context of the post-9/11 "war on terrorism." The *Buffalo News*, for example, wrote:

> A recent story in the *Washington Post* makes clear what every American must have already suspected regarding the treatment of al-Qaida and Taliban prisoners. Harsh treatment, perhaps to the point of torture. For the most part, we're not losing sleep over that revelation, given the facts of the last 15 months. But while aggressive interrogation techniques are both important and even, to a point, acceptable, there still must be rules and mechanisms for accountability to prevent wholesale torture.[16]

Some of the media's chosen experts were enthusiastic advocates of wholesale torture and vilified the opponents of this interrogation method. Thus, law professor emeritus Henry Mark Holzer wrote:

> There are those among us—Jimmy Carter-like pacifists and Ramsey Clark-type America haters come to mind—who would probably stand by idly and endure

an atomic holocaust. But most people would doubtless opt for torture, albeit reluctantly. These realists—and I suspect they are a large majority of the American public—would be correct. In approving the use of torture—or at least accepting it—they needn't suffer even a scintilla of moral guilt. Torture of whatever kind, and no matter how brutal, in defense of human rights and legitimate self-preservation is not only not immoral; it is a moral imperative.[17]

Bill O'Reilly, the host of *The O'Reilly Factor* on Fox News, did not openly endorse all-out torture but said it would be "foolish" to give captured terrorists any rights under the Geneva Convention. He argued that terrorists "deserve nothing. In most other societies, they would have already been executed. Short of torture, military interrogators are entitled to do whatever's necessary to exact information from these people." He never specified his understanding of torture, and the words "short of torture" and "whatever's necessary to extract information."

Average citizens, when given a rare opportunity by the media, were far more restrained and engaged in thoughtful debate. The following excerpts are taken from the remarks of two citizens who spoke in support of and in opposition to torture during a town hall meeting in New York City that was broadcast by *Nightline* and moderated by Ted Koppel:

Mr. Casey: I live down in Rockaway. And for those of you who know Rockaway, we lost 70 people from my little town in—in the Trade Center collapse. . . . The—you know, you talk about torturing them [terrorists]. If—if they could have gotten these people that flew those tra—planes into the World Trade Center and had been able to get that information from them beforehand, I think a lot of people around here would have been a lot happier, and we wouldn't have all the grief that we have here.

Koppel: Well . . .

Mr. Casey: And I—I don't—I—I feel there should be limits, but I—I think the limits should—I don't think it should be that extreme. I think there should be controls on it, but if you can get the information out of them, I think you should have to get it.

Ms. Mary Fontana: Hi, my name is Mary Fontana. I lost my husband Dave, who was a firefighter in Brooklyn and he also—his father was a vet and his uncle was killed in the Battle of the Bulge. I think it's—we have to—it's a slippery slope to start to think about our rights in this country, the rights that he died for and the rights that his father and uncle did. . . . So I think that, you know, you really have to be careful about who we begin to target because I think it will be—create prejudice, and it will start to become a witch hunt really—that's my concern that, you know, we all live in this country. My husband died for our rights to live together, and that we really have to be careful when we start talking about torturing people for information. It's frightening to me.[18]

These two town hall participants and all the others that spoke out during the event were aware of the risks and benefits inherent in the trade-off between civil liberties and security. They did not attack opposing viewpoints. For the most part, the pro and con views expressed in letters-to-the-editor were equally thoughtful and—civil.

All in all, expert advocates of torture, torture lite, coercion, or other "exceptional" interrogation methods were prominently and frequently represented in television news and talk programs and on the op-ed pages of newspapers in the two and a half years after 9/11. In Ted Koppel's electronic town hall meeting, on the other hand, the opponents of torture had a ten-to-four advantage over the supporters. Assuming that the citizens who got a chance to voice their opinions were randomly selected, there is no way to know how many in the audience were supporting and rejecting the torturing of terrorists and suspected terrorists.

THE PUBLIC AND TORTURE BEFORE
THE ABU GHRAIB REVELATIONS

In the first phase of the torture debate, which ended with the pictorial disclosure of the gross human rights violations at Abu Ghraib, some supporters of various forms of torture claimed to have popular support on their side. Henry Mark Holzer wrote that "most people would doubtless opt for torture, albeit reluctantly."[19] But such claims were not borne out by actual public opinion surveys or polling opinion but based on what Robert Entman has called "perceived public opinion." According to Entman,

> Perceived opinion is the general sense of the public's opinions that is held by most observers, including journalists and politicians, and members of the public themselves. This is a convenient fiction observers use to characterize the comprehensive preferences of a majority of citizens. . . .
> Polling opinion and perceived public opinion may or may not be identical, because politicians and journalists frequently ignore survey results, in part because the data are so often inconclusive and in part because neglecting polls can be strategically useful. Instead, they just declaim about what the American people allegedly believe—and they can usually find a poll somewhere to support them.[20]

Contrary to what some of the experts claimed in the media, representative public opinion surveys revealed that the American public was divided on the issue of torture, that there was not at all a clear majority in favor of torturing terrorists. Instead, just a few weeks after 9/11, in early October 2001, a Gallup/CNN/*USA Today* survey found that 45 percent of the public supported and 53 percent opposed the torture of terrorists. A Fox/Opinion

Dynamics poll in March 2002 showed 41 percent of the public supportive of and 47 percent opposed to torturing terrorists; a year later a second poll by the same organizations showed that 44 percent of the public favored and 42 percent opposed torture as an interrogation method. Considering the margins of error, these three polls established that the American public was split down the middle on this issue—although it was obvious that the survey in March of 2003 showed for the first time a slight plurality of Americans supporting the torture of terrorists. However slight, this attitudinal change came after the arrest of Al Qaeda operative Khalid Sheikh Mohammed and during a period when the issue of torture received a great deal of media attention and protorture voices outscored antitorture voices in the media—especially in television (See also table 5.1). As for the two Fox News/Opinion Dynamics polls, it is noteworthy that nearly one-fourth of the respondents who said they opposed the torture of terrorist suspects to extract information in their responses to the first question, changed their minds and approved of the method if it was possible to save a member of their own family.

An *Investor's Business Daily/Christian Science Monitor* poll in early November 2001, on the other hand, showed that one-third of the public approved of torture and two-thirds rejected this method. In other words, this result reflected strong opposition to torture and was very different from the outcomes of the three other surveys—most likely because respondents reacted to different question wordings. In the Gallup/CNN/*USA Today* and Fox/Opinion Dynamics surveys the participants were explicitly asked about their positions on torturing terrorists to get information about future attacks.

Table 5.1.   U.S. Public Opinion on the Torture of Terrorists/Suspected Terrorists before the Abu Ghraib Revelations

	Support (%)	Oppose (%)	Depends/D.K/N. Sure (%)
Gallup/CNN/*USA Today*			
10/5–10/6, 2001	45	53	3
Investor's Business Daily/Christian Science			
11/7–11/11, 2001	32	66	3
Fox News/Opinion Dynamics			
3/12–3/13, 2002	41	47	12
Fox News/Opinion Dynamics			
3/12–3/13, 2003	44	42	14
Outsourcing Torture			
ABC News			
9/4–9/7, 2003	23	73	3

The *Investor's Daily/Christian Science Monitor* poll, on the other hand, asked respondents more broadly to envision a scenario in which they could support (or not support) the torture of terrorists at home or abroad. In this case there was no reference to torture for the sake of gaining information to prevent future terrorism. Perhaps this poll reflected also the American public's opposition to asking foreign government agents to torture terrorists on America's behalf. This opposition was strongly expressed when ABC News conducted a survey in September 2003 that asked respondents whether they supported or opposed the U.S. government's arranging for foreign security personnel to torture terrorists abroad in order to extract information.

As a guest on the *Today Show*, Alan Dershowitz claimed that "the vast majority of Americans, when asked on various TV shows would favor torture if we had a ticking bomb terrorist case."[21] It is inconceivable that Professor Dershowitz would not know that instant polls on TV shows are not at all reflective of what the American public collectively thinks. Indeed, when CNN asked the audience of one program whether Khalid Sheikh Mohammed should be tortured into telling whatever he knows, more than half of the respondents were in favor of interrogators' using torture.[22] The result was similar when AOL asked a comparable question and invited audience members to express their preferences.[23]

Protorture sentiment was found on several Internet sites. For example, *e.thePeople* asked visitors, "Should we (the USA) torture terrorists for information?" 59 percent responded with yes, 41 percent with no.[24] 49 percent of the respondents to an online poll by *Crimeweek Daily* approved of torturing terrorists under all circumstances (to prevent upcoming acts, to get the names of other terrorists, and to obtain confessions); 9 percent approved only to obtain information that could prevent upcoming terrorist attacks; 7 percent were in favor of torture in order to prevent upcoming terrorist acts and to get the names of other terrorists; only 33 percent chose the "never" option, indicating that they would not approve of torture under any circumstance.[25] In spite of such polls' randomness and their openness to manipulation by organized interests, they were used by proponents of one or the other form of torture to claim that the majority of Americans supported their position.

THE ABU GHRAIB TORTURE
SCANDAL AND ITS IMPACT

Early on, when Amnesty International and other sources pointed to gross mistreatment of terrorists and suspected terrorists in detention facilities under U.S. control, even leading elite media organizations paid little or no attention. As the *Columbia Journalism Review* put it,

Scattered reports last summer and fall [2003] by the AP, Reuters, *The Washington Post*, and others alluded to mistreatment of prisoners, but none suggested the story's magnitude. Traditionally, Red Cross dossiers on breaches of the Geneva Convention are secret, as a condition of the group's access to military prisons. But given the degree of the organization's frustration over all those months, it is surprising that little or nothing of the Red Cross's findings made its way into the press. Amnesty International, meanwhile, was under no such stricture and was putting out press releases. One, in July 2003, cited "reports of torture" by coalition forces.[26]

Moreover, there were confidential reports based on investigations by U.S. military officers that documented the mistreatment of Iraqi prisoners and serious violations of international law months before the Abu Ghraib story broke without the media "watchdog" getting wind of them in a timely fashion. According to the *Columbia Journalism Review*, "had editors around the country and elsewhere listened a bit more carefully . . . to the clear signals, they might—just possibly—have saved the lives of some Iraqis and prevented the torment of others. . . . But regrettably and unnecessarily, the facts lay at the outer edge of journalism's radar screen for too long."[27]

Because the press "watchdog" slept, for many, probably most Americans, the mass-mediated public debate surrounding the pros and cons of torturing terrorists was abstract, a theoretical exercise—until CBS News on *60 Minutes II* and Seymour Hersh in *The New Yorker* showed pictures of and described the unspeakably inhuman treatment of Iraqi detainees by U.S. soldiers at Abu Ghraib prison. The most shocking revelations were based on a report by Major General Antonio M. Taguba and on the pictures shot by the Abu Ghraib perpetrators themselves.

While the news media did report on Abu Ghraib and "alleged abuses" or "abuses" in U.S. detention facilities at Guantanamo Bay and elsewhere, the coverage was in many instances less prominent and less durable than the shocking material deserved. Michael Getler, the ombudsman of the *Washington Post*, for example, asked why the editors of the *Post* did not put the story on the front page once it had been reported by CBS News and the *New Yorker*. Obviously, decision making in many American newsrooms was affected by fears of contributing to a global backlash and of being criticized as unpatriotic at home.

To be sure, voices that condemned the torturous treatment of prisoners were heard in news accounts—especially when they belonged to Republicans and supporters of the George W. Bush administration. For example, when U.S. Senator Lindsey Graham (R-South Carolina) said that the "American public needs to understand we are talking about rape and murder," he got plenty of media attention, as did other Washingtonians who expressed shock and outrage.[28] In an op-ed article in the *New York Times*, Donald P. Gregg, national security advisor to George H. W. Bush from 1989 to 1993, criticized the lawyers in the George W. Bush administration for "pushing aside longstanding prohibitions on the use of torture by Americans."[29]

But even as more visuals of the dark happenings at Abu Ghraib were shown on television screens, on the Internet, and in print, the news also paid a great deal of attention to those who denied and downplayed "wrongdoings" and, in fact, attacked the critics of torture practices. Thus, U.S. Senator James Inhofe (R-Oklahoma) made the news when he declared that he "had heard enough from critics of the prisoner abuse" and added the made-for-broadcasters sound bite that he was "outraged by the outrage."[30] Rush Limbaugh got media attention when he compared the torturous treatment of Iraqi inmates to hazing practices on college campuses, saying that what the soldiers at Abu Ghraib did was "no different than what happens at the Skull & Bones initiation." According to news accounts, Limbaugh added, "I am talking about people having a good time. You ever heard of emotional release? You ever heard of [the] need to blow some steam off?"[31] Even those who characterized the Abu Ghraib horror pictures as staged and faked got the attention of some reporters.[32]

AVOIDING THE T-WORD

Whereas the American news media had no problem using the term "torture" in the hypothetical debate before the Abu Ghraib revelations, members of the fourth estate were terribly reluctant to use the T-word once they had shown and the public had seen the graphic scenes of actual torture at the Iraqi detention facility. While it may be entirely possible that news organizations did not want to believe that Americans were torturers before the Abu Ghraib story broke, the pictorial proof of actual torture did away with any doubts. Yet, an ironic consequence of the Abu Ghraib revelations was the drastic decline of the use of the T-word in pertinent news accounts. Instead, anchors, correspondents, and reporters themselves preferred terms like "abuse," "alleged abuse," "mistreatment," and "wrongdoing." As Susan Sontag wrote in her essay "Regarding the Torture of Others,"

> There was also the avoidance of the word "torture" [on the part of the Bush administration]. The prisoners had possibly been the objects of "abuse," eventually of "humiliation"—that was the most to be admitted. "My impression is that what has been charged thus far is abuse, which I believe technically is different from torture," Secretary of Defense Donald Rumsfeld said at a press conference. "And therefore I'm not going to address the 'torture' word."[33]

It seemed that the news media took their cue from the defense secretary's linguistic skills. As table 5.2 shows, in the year following the breaking news

Table 5.2.   Terms Used by Major News Organizations in Reports on the Abu Ghraib Torture Scandal (May 1, 2004–April 30, 2005)

	abuse and torture (N)	abuse only (N)	torture only (N)
ABC News	43	115	—
CBS News	42	118	13
NBC News	35	151	7
N.Y. Times	179	508	144
Wash. Post	193	380	37

N = Number of broadcast segments or newspaper stories

of the Abu Ghraib scandal, the three major television networks and two of the country's leading elite newspapers chose the term "abuse" far more often than "torture" in stories about Abu Ghraib. ABC News aired 158 pertinent stories that contained the term "abuse," and 43 of these stories mentioned both "abuse" and "torture." So a total of 115 segments mentioned only "abuse" in the context of Abu Ghraib and none referred solely to "torture." The linguistic choices were very similar at CBS News and NBC News. Thus, CBS News broadcast 160 stories that mentioned "abuse" and 55 containing "torture," but while 118 news segments used the term "abuse" only, just 13 mentioned "torture" only. NBC News used the term "abuse" in a total of 186 news segments, "torture" in merely 35 stories. More importantly, the network aired 151 stories with the term "abuse" only and just 7 that contained the T-word only.

During the same time period, the print media, too, chose the term "abuse" far more often than "torture" in the context of Abu Ghraib. For example, whereas only 144 articles in the *New York Times* mentioned "torture" and not "abuse," 508 news items contained the word "abuse" and not "torture." Similarly, the *Washington Post* published ten times more stories that mentioned "abuse" and not "torture" (380) in the context of Abu Ghraib than articles containing the term "torture" only (37).

Equally revealing was the reluctance of the print press to use the term "torture" in headlines above stories dealing with the Abu Ghraib case. In the year following the Abu Ghraib revelations, the *New York Times*, for example, carried 42 news items with the word "torture" in their headlines and "Abu Ghraib" in the full text. Of these, 24 were letters-to-the-editor, one was an editorial, another one an essay on torture by Susan Sontag, and three were book reviews dealing with volumes on Abu Ghraib and torture. Thus, only 13 news articles that mentioned Abu Ghraib in the full text used the T-word in the headlines. Conversely, of the 130 news items that mentioned "abuse" in their headlines, 12 were letters-to-the editor and one was an editorial, so that 117 pertinent straight news stories contained the term "abuse" in the headlines.

But while these results of the quantitative analysis are revealing, they do not tell the whole story of the media's avoidance of the T-word. Even investigative reporter Seymour Hersh was very careful in his linguistic choices when he wrote his initial Abu Ghraib story. While Hersh's article carried the headline "Torture at Abu Ghraib," a title that was presumably picked by his editors, the author himself characterized what was done to detainees as "wrongdoing" and "abuse"—not torture. When the T-word was mentioned, Hersh referred to the "torture and weekly executions" at Abu Ghraib during Saddam Hussein's reign of terror, a quote by a professor of Middle Eastern studies, and the findings in General Taguba's report. In this respect, the reporting patterns of the media at large mirrored the trailblazing article in the *New Yorker*. In most instances, anchors, correspondents, and reporters themselves did not speak or write of "torture" in the context of the Abu Ghraib scandal but left this characterization to named or unnamed sources that were critical of the treatment of detainees by Americans. A case in point was the *CBS Evening News* on April 29, 2004: in introducing the story about the U.S. Army's response "to documented mistreatment of Iraqi prisoners by American soldiers," Dan Rather himself speaks of "mistreatment" and "abuses." In the following correspondent report, David Martin refers to "Iraqi prisoners mistreated and humiliated by their American jailers." He mentions the T-word only in the context of "the Abu Ghraib Prison outside Baghdad, once infamous under Saddam Hussein as a place of torture and death." Or take the *NBC Nightly News* of May 7, 2004. In introducing the "Iraqi prisoner abuse scandal," anchor Brian Williams asked, "What were military superiors told about the abuse and when were they told?" In the following report, after speaking of "abuses" and "abuse," Lisa Myers mentions that the International Red Cross warned the U.S. government of the "widespread abuse" of detainees "tantamount to torture."

Typically, broadcasts contained the term "torture" when President George W. Bush and others in the administration denied that they approved the torturing of terrorists and enemy combatants or when administration officials released documents that supported these denials. The following excerpt from ABC's *World News Tonight with Peter Jennings* on June 22, 2004 illustrates this pattern:

Peter Jennings: The White House today produced a huge number of documents for reporters about torture. The president and other members of the administration have been accused by many of their critics of condoning torture in the war against terrorism, at Abu Ghraib prison in Iraq, at Guantanamo Bay and other places less in the news. Our White House correspondent Terry Moran has been looking at the paperwork this afternoon, and there was a lot of it, Terry.

Terry Moran: President Bush declared unequivocally that he has not and will not order a detainee to be tortured.

President George W. Bush: I have never ordered torture. I will never order torture.

Leading newspapers used the T-word in straight news stories mostly, when the term was mentioned in defense of the Bush administration. This was even more so with respect to headlines. Thus, of the few pertinent headlines in the *New York Times* that contained the T-word, the following were typical: "Ashcroft says the White House never authorized tactics breaking laws on torture" (June 9, 2004); "U.S. spells out new definition curbing torture" (January 1, 2005); "Bush's counsel sought ruling about torture" (January 5, 2005); "Gonzales speaks against torture during hearing" (January 7, 2005). On the other hand, the editorial page editors of the *Times* were far less reluctant to resort to the T-word in headlines of the letters-to-the-editor sections and their own opinion pieces. Shortly after the Abu Ghraib scandal broke, for example, the *Times* published an editorial under the headline "The Torture Photos" that stated,

> It seems gloomily possible that in years to come, when people in the Middle East recall the invasion of Iraq, they will speak not of the lost American lives or the toppling of a brutal dictator. The most enduring image of the occupation may be those pictures of grinning American soldiers torturing Iraqi prisoners.[34]

Obviously, however, these pictures were not enduring enough for television network news to follow up on related developments or cover the military trials of defendants accused of the Abu Ghraib cruelties extensively. As *New York Times* columnist Frank Rich wrote after the defense rested in the trial of Specialist Charles A. Graner Jr. for the torture practices at Abu Ghraib,

> A not so funny thing happened to the Graner case on its way to trial. Since the early bomb shells from Abu Ghraib last year, the torture story has all but vanished from television, even as there have been continued revelations in the major newspapers and magazines like The New Yorker, the New York Review of Books and Vanity Fair. If a story is not on TV in America, it doesn't exist in our culture.
>
> The minimizing—and in some cases outright elimination—of Abu Ghraib and its aftermath from network news coverage is in part (but only in part) political. Fox News, needless to say, has trivialized the story from the get-go, as hallmarked by Bill O'Reilly's proud refusal to run the photos of Graner & Company after they first surfaced at CBS.
>
> Since the election [and the reelection of President George W. Bush], some news organizations, most conspicuously NBC, have seemed eager to rally around the winner and avoid discouraging words of any kind.[35]

But while the television networks lost interest in Abu Ghraib and similar crime stories after the flow of new "abuse" pictures stopped, they had broadcast and rebroadcast the horror pictures initially. And since most

Americans rely on television news for their political information, the vast majority of the public knew about Abu Ghraib. When asked by pollsters in the weeks after the torture story broke whether they happened to follow news reports of prisoner abuse in Iraq involving U.S. soldiers, 76 percent of the respondents in one survey, 71 percent in a second poll, and 83 percent in yet another survey said that they had followed the story "very closely" or "closely"; only 4 percent, 9 percent, and 6 percent respectively chose the "not at all closely" option.[36] Since about three of four Americans followed this particular news story very closely or closely, one wonders what kind of opinions the public formed on the basis of what they learned exclusively from news accounts.

PUBLIC OPINION AFTER ABU GHRAIB

Just as the news media seemed uncomfortable in using the T-word to describe the treatment of Iraqi inmates at Abu Ghraib prison, survey organizations, too, used "abuse" far more often than "torture" in questions relating to the fate of prisoners in Iraq. Thus, the IPOLL archive of the Roper Center for Public Opinion Research at the University of Connecticut listed eighty relevant questions mentioning only "abuse" relating to the treatment of prisoners versus ten referring just to "torture." Not surprisingly, the majority of Americans felt that what occurred at Abu Ghraib was "abuse" rather than "torture." When asked a few weeks after being exposed to the Abu Ghraib visuals, "Do you think what American soldiers did to prisoners at the Abu Ghraib prison in Baghdad amounts to torture, or do you think it was abuse, but not torture?", 60 percent said it was "abuse but not torture," while only 29 percent felt it was "torture." The same survey found that 35 percent of the public found the torture of suspected terrorists to be "acceptable in some cases," while 63 percent of respondents said that torture is never acceptable. Yet, 46 percent said that physical abuse short of torture is acceptable in some of these cases, and just 52 percent felt that physical abuse is never acceptable. With the pictures of the Abu Ghraib scandal fresh in mind, 51 percent of Americans believed that the U.S. government "as a matter of policy" was using "torture" in the war against terrorism, while 43 percent did not think so. However, 66 percent thought that it was U.S. policy to use "physical abuse" in fighting terrorists, and 29 percent did not believe so.[37]

When asked about specific methods designed to get information from suspected terrorists, a majority of Americans approved of depriving detainees of sleep, bombarding them with loud noise for long periods of time, and keeping hoods over their heads, but rejected other measures, such as threatening family members, applying electric shock, or holding heads under water. Still, it is disconcerting that sizeable minorities were supportive of threatening to shoot a suspect (41 percent), exposing him to extreme heat and cold (40 percent), withholding food and water (38 percent), punching and kicking him (29 percent), making the prisoner go naked (25 percent), and holding a suspect's head under water (21 percent).[38] Moreover, as memories of the Abu Ghraib torture pictures faded, Americans were less inclined to agree with the statement that torture is "never justified" as a means to force suspected terrorists to reveal important information. By December 2004, more than seven months after the Abu Ghraib story broke, only 27 percent of the public rejected the torture of terrorist suspects categorically, while 69 percent found it justified to varying degrees, namely "often" (15 percent), "sometimes" (30 percent), or "rarely" (24 percent). But although the majority of Americans believed, as mentioned above, that the mistreatment of prisoners at Abu Ghraib was "abuse," not "torture," pollsters did not ask whether respondents found the "abuse" of suspected terrorists justified or not.

The bottom line is simply this: while most Americans were aware of what had happened at Abu Ghraib and one in three claimed to be "angry" about the "apparent abuse" of prisoners by U.S. soldiers, there was no public outrage. As Joseph Lelyveld reported,

> Members of Congress say they receive a negligible number of letters and calls about the revelations that keep coming. "You asked whether they want it clear or want it blurred," Senator Susan Collins, a Maine Republican, said to me about the reactions of her constituents to the torture allegations that alarm her. "I think they want it blurry."[39]

In early 2005, the *New York Times* condemned the outsourcing of torture to countries with histories of human rights violations, a practice known as "extraordinary rendition" or simply "rendition" in intelligence circles. "Let's be clear about this," the editorial stated, "Any prisoner of the United States is protected by American values. That cannot be changed by sending him to another country and pretending not to notice that he's being tortured."[40] Unfortunately, just as most of the media failed to report timely on the torture in U.S.-controlled prisons abroad, they were late in focusing on and criticizing the outsourcing of torture—although some news organizations did publish such stories. As Sanford Levinson, a professor of law at the University of Texas Law School, wrote after the Abu Ghraib torture scandal broke,

> For example, on December 26, 2002, The Washington Post published an extensive report on the appalling treatment of prisoners and detainees in Afghanistan, including "rendering" to other countries. "We don't kick the [expletive] out of them," one anonymous U.S. official was quoted as saying. "We

send them to other countries so they can kick the [expletive] out of them." Similar stories appeared in such outlets as The New York Times and The Economist. None appears to have had the slightest impact. The Economist in January 2003 described the American discussion of allegations of torture as "desultory."[41]

Levinson was right in suggesting that there was no excuse for decision-makers in Washington and for everyone who read such stories to simply go on "with our lives as if they had nothing to do with us and concerned only the various 'others' living in strange and faraway places."[42] Instead, Levinson concluded,

Why, then, should we feign shock "that inexperienced, frightened, and foolish—it is almost pointless to view them as "evil"—young soldiers would have had little or no understanding of what the limits were on what they could do? They have received not the slightest trace of genuine leadership on the issue.[43]

While it is certainly true that the available news reports didn't have any impact in terms of putting the torture issue high onto the public agenda, the media's failure to report frequently, prominently, and—most of all—critically on this dark chapter in the war on terrorism may have encouraged the proponents and practitioners of abuse, coercion, torture lite, and hard-core torture.

DEHUMANIZING THE ENEMY

In early 2003, after the capture of Khalid Sheikh Mohammed (KSM), a close associate of Osama bin Laden, Jack Wheeler of the Freedom Research Foundation appeared as a guest on the Fox News *Hannity & Colmes* program. When Alan Colmes asked, "Tell us what you want to do to this guy," Dr. Wheeler answered, "Whatever is necessary to extract the information that he has out of his brain. And I mean whatever is necessary." Later in the program, the expert guest said in an exchange with host Sean Hannity, "I don't care what you do to him. This man is a piece of human garbage." Hannity's answer: "Well I agree with that."[44]

Following on the heels of the Abu Ghraib torture scandal, Rush Limbaugh said on his radio program in reaction to the news of the brutal beheading of the American Nicholas Berg by his kidnappers in Iraq,

They're the ones who are sick. They're the ones who are perverted. They are the ones who are dangerous. They are the ones who are subhuman debris, not the United States of America and not our soldiers and not our prison guards.[45]

Around the same time, a former CIA operative said in a discussion of interrogation methods on the *Hannity & Colmes* program,

We catch an al Qaeda member, we knows [*sic*] he's al Qaeda, his life as he knows it has got to be over.

Listen, I lived with these animals. This is a sub-human species of somehow a deviation of the human, of the true human. They care for nothing. They kill everything in their path. All bets are off. This is an animal that's unlike any we've ever faced.[46]

In an ironic way, the preachers of hate have a great deal in common with terrorists in that both sell the "us" against "them" divide. With respect to terrorists, Ehud Sprinzak has described a process of moral disengagement at the end of which the enemies "are depersonalized and dehumanized. They are derogated to the ranks of subhuman species. Dehumanization makes it possible for the radicals to be disengaged morally and to commit atrocities without a second thought."[47] For terrorists, part of the moral disengagement process has long been the practice of comparing their targets to animals, calling them "pigs" or "dogs," and consequently harming them. To the extent that the enemy in the "war on terrorism" was perceived by Americans as "garbage," "debris," and "subhuman," this moral disengagement paved the way for the inhumane treatment of detainees.

One American soldier, an M.P. who had worked at Abu Ghraib prison, for example, testified that on one occasion one of the guards, Sergeant Ivan L. Frederick II, had pointed at two naked detainees who were forced to masturbate. "Look what these animals do when you leave them alone for two seconds," he said.[48] According to his sworn statement, one detainee recalled that "they forced us to walk like dogs on our hands and knees. And we had to bark like a dog and if we didn't do that, they start hitting us hard on our face and chest with no mercy."[49] There was also the publicized photograph of a naked prisoner at Abu Ghraib held like a dog at a leash by an American female guard.

Such distinct efforts to dehumanize prisoners were not limited to the Iraqi prison. The following entry in the interrogation log of Mohammed al-Qahtani, believed to have been the designated twentieth hijacker in the 9/11 terrorist attacks and held in the Guantanamo Bay prison, reveals that the Al Qaeda member was considered even less than an animal: "Told detainee that a dog is held in higher esteem [than he] because dogs know right from wrong, and know how to protect innocent people from bad people. Began teaching the detainee lessons such as stay, come, and bark to elevate his social status up to that of a dog."[50]

After Anthony Lewis wrote about this utterly inhuman treatment of prisoners in an op-ed article in the *New York Times*, one reader, in his published letter-to-the-editor, challenged Lewis's condemnation of human rights violations. "The prisoners held in Guantanamo are without rights because of their choice to fight without any government's protection. Americans have no reason to protect them. As our enemies, they are lucky even to be alive."[51] But another reader pointed to the essence of torturous practices when he wrote, "What becomes of our young people in the military who are asked or commanded to do the unspeakable to another human being? Torturers seek to dehumanize the prisoner, but in fact, it is they who lose their humanity."[52]

VILIFYING THE ENEMY'S
RELIGION AND RELIGIOUS PRACTICES

Shortly after 9/11, President George W. Bush, New York's Mayor Rudy Giuliani, and other leaders went public to urge Americans not to blame all Muslims and not to blame Islam for what some terrorists did in the name of their religion. But rather quickly, these voices went for the most part silent. Given today's information glut, the mass media, especially television, tend to pay more attention to the loudest and most outrageous statements rather than to the calm voices of reason—except when the latter belong to prominent leaders. Thus, after 9/11, those who vilified the religious practices of Muslims and their religion far too often received media attention without being taken to task for their bigotry.

After the capture of Khalid Sheikh Mohammed (KSM), one of the known Al Qaeda leaders, the *Washington Times* published on op-ed article by Jack Wheeler of the Freedom Research Foundation that described in gruesome details the kind of torture that would make KSM "sing in an hour."[53] He clearly was out to violate all the sensibilities of Mohammed that were related to his Islamic faith. Wheeler suggested the Al Qaeda terrorist should be injected with a drug that would paralyze his breathing muscles but not affect his central nervous system and his ability to think and answer questions. He should be put on a mechanical respirator without which he would suffocate and die. After these preliminaries, Wheeler described the interrogation of KSM this way:

> Now the interrogation begins. KSM is asked a series of questions to which the answers are known [e.g., Are you a Muslim? Would you like a drink of pig grease?]. If he lies, the respirator is turned off. Few experiences are more terrifying than that of suffocation. After a sufficiently terrifying period of suffocation, the respirator is turned back on, the question is asked again, and the process repeats itself until he tells the truth.
>
> After all useful information has been extracted from his brain, KSM should be informed that he will now be killed after his body is smeared with pig fat, that his dead body will be handled by women, and all actions taken that prevent a Muslim from entering heaven upon death so that he dies believing he

will never get the heavenly wine and virgins, but will burn in Hell instead. Upon his execution, there should be no physical remains. The body should be cremated and the ashes scattered to the winds.[54]

Wheeler's remarks were particularly extreme, but the news media reported on other rhetorical attacks on Muslims and their religion. The Reverend Franklin Graham, who delivered the benediction at George W. Bush's first presidential inauguration, said, for example, "Islam as a whole is evil." And, "It wasn't Methodists flying into those buildings, and it wasn't Lutherans. It was an attack on this country by people of Islamic faith."[55] *NBC Nightly News* anchor Tom Brokaw introduced the news segment that reported Graham's remarks by telling his audience that "one of the president's close friends in the American religious establishment has had some very harsh words for the Muslim faith." One wonders how the maligning of the whole religion of Islam could be described simply as having "some very harsh words."

As *World News Tonight with Peter Jennings* reported, Franklin Graham had plenty of company among leading evangelical preachers when it came to vilifying Muslims and Islam, as the following excerpts from the broadcast demonstrated:

Pat Robertson, Televangelist: Adolph [*sic*] Hitler was bad. But what the Muslims want to do to Jews is worse.

Jerry Falwell, Televangelist: I think Mohammed is a terrorist.

Reverend Jerry Vines, Evangelist: Islam was founded by Mohammed, a demon-possessed pedophile who had twelve wives, and his last one was a nine-year-old girl.

Jimmy Swaggart, Televangelist: We ought to take, we ought to take every single Muslim student in every college in this nation and ship them back to where they came from.

At the end of the segment, anchorman Jennings told his audience benignly, "This is a delicate subject, as you know."[56] He invited the audience to voice their opinions on the program's web site.

While President Bush assured viewers on the same broadcast mildly that "some of the comments that have been uttered about Islam do not reflect the sentiments of my government or the sentiments of the American people,"[57] Franklin Graham was invited in the spring of 2003 and after his insult of Islam to lead Good Friday services at the Pentagon—in spite of objections by Muslim employees. Similarly, after Army Lt. General William G. Boykin, one of the top generals at the Pentagon, told church groups repeatedly that the enemy in the war on terrorism was "Satan," he was not reprimanded by his superiors.

These attacks not only disparaged Muslims abroad but vilified Muslim Americans as well—sometimes even explicitly. On CNN, the Reverend Anis Shorrosh, introduced as "a Christian theologian who has ministered in the Middle East," suggested that "theologically a Muslim cannot be a true patriotic American citizen, because his allegiance is to Allah, the Moon [*sic*] God of Arabia."[58]

It may never be known whether and how these messages and the absence of equally prominent rebuttals in the news influenced the practitioners of torture and their enablers. There is no doubt that investigations into the abuse, torture, and death of detainees at Abu Ghraib and elsewhere uncovered treatment patterns aimed at degrading Muslim inmates' faith and violating the well-known sensitivities of Muslims and Arabs. In his sworn testimony, one Abu Ghraib prisoner described unspeakably sadistic brutalities and the following attacks on his religion and the precepts of Islam:

> They ordered me to curse Islam and because they started to hit my broken leg, I cursed my religion. They ordered me to thank Jesus that I'm alive. And I did what they ordered me. This is against my belief.
> They forced me to eat pork and they put liquor in my mouth.[59]

Tony Judt noted that many of the interrogation techniques used at U.S. detention centers abroad "will be familiar to students of Eastern Europe in the Fifties or Latin America in the Seventies and Eighties."[60] But, as Judt added, "American interrogators have also innovated. One technique has been forcibly to wrap suspects—and their Korans—in Israeli flags."[61] No doubt, another measure to mock the detainees' religious convictions and respect for the Koran.

Describing the human rights violations at Abu Ghraib as described in General Taguba's report and depicted in the photographs taken by the "wrongdoers," Seymour Hersh wrote, "Yet another photograph shows a kneeling, naked, unhooded male prisoner, head momentarily turned away from the camera, posed to make it appear that he is performing oral sex on another male prisoner, who is naked and hooded."[62] Hersh left no doubt about the aim and impact of these and many similar "abuses":

> Such dehumanization is unacceptable in any culture, but it is especially so in the Arab world. Homosexual acts are against Islamic law and it is humiliating for men to be naked in front of other men. Bernard Haykel, a professor of Middle Eastern Studies at New York University explained, "Being put on top of each other and forced to masturbate, being naked in front of each other—it's all a form of torture."[63]

A year later, as even some conservative Republicans inside and outside of Congress called for an independent investigation into the "allegations" surrounding the Guantanamo Bay detainees and gave otherwise compliant news organizations cover to report prominently on alleged physical abuse and the desecration of the Koran, the administration and its supporters denied any wrongdoing. As Vice President Dick Cheney said on the "Larry King Live" infotainment show on CNN, the detainees at Guantanamo Bay have been "well treated, treated humanely and decently."[64]

Responding to the release of the Italian movie *The Battle of Algiers* in the early 1970s that documented the use of torture in Algeria under his command, French general Jacques Massu called this interrogation method "a cruel necessity."[65] He made the same argument that American advocates of torture used in the war on terrorism, namely, that the bad guys are far more brutal than we, the good guys, are. Thus, General Massu wrote:

> I am not afraid of the word torture, but I think in the majority of cases, the French military men obliged to use it to vanquish terrorism were, fortunately, choir boys compared with the use to which it was put by the rebels. The latter's extreme savagery led us to some ferocity, it is certain, but we remained within the law of eye for eye, tooth for tooth.[66]

Three decades later, near the end of his life, the general had a change of heart and, as recalled at the time of his death in 2002, stated that "Torture is not indispensable in time of war, we could have gotten along without it very well." He also said, "Morally torture is something very ugly."[67] While, according to news accounts, the film *The Battle of Algiers* was screened at the Pentagon after the fall of Saddam Hussein's regime, it might have been better to have everyone read the general's obituary.

NOTES

1. The town hall meeting was held and broadcast on *Nightline*, ABC, on March 8, 2002.

2. *World News Tonight with Peter Jennings*, ABC, March 4, 2003.

3. Mark Mcguire, "Good guys are doing bad things this season," *Times Union* (Albany, New York), January 14, 2003, D1.

4. Thompson, the director of the Center for the Study of Popular Television at Syracuse University, was quoted in Mcguire, "Good guys are doing bad things this season."

5. Joseph Lelyveld, "Interrogating Ourselves," *New York Times Magazine*, June 12, 2005, 35.

6. For an excellent study on the longer-term impact of television on its audiences see James Shanahan and Michael Morgan, *Television and Its Viewers: Cultivation Theory and Research* (New York: Cambridge University Press, 1999).

7. Stuart Taylor Jr., "Is it ever right to torture suspected terrorists?" *National Journal*, March 8, 2003.

8. Jonathan Alter, "Time to think about torture," *Newsweek*, November 5, 2001, 45.

9. Mark Bowden, "The dark art of interrogation," *Atlantic Monthly*, October 2003, 53.

10. Bowden, "The dark art of interrogation," 76.

11. Philip B. Heymann, *Terrorism, Freedom, and Security: Winning Without War* (Cambridge, MA: MIT Press, 2003), 111.

12. Jonathan Turley, "Rights on the Rack; Alleged torture in terror war imperils U.S. standards of humanity," *Los Angeles Times*, March 6, 2003, B17.

13. Richard Cohen, "Using torture to fight terror," *Washington Post*, March 6, 2003, A23.

14. "Torture is not an option," *Washington Post*, December 27, 2002, A24.

15. "Answers about torture," *Washington Post*, March 16, 2003, B6.

16. "A question of torture," *Buffalo News*, December 30, 2002, B8.

17. Henry Mark Holzer, "Terrorism interrogations and torture," *Milwaukee Journal Sentinel*, March 16, 2003, 5J.

18. From *Nightline*, ABC, March 8, 2002.

19. Holzer, "Terrorism interrogations and torture."

20. Robert M. Entman, "Declarations of Independence: The Growth of Media Power after the Cold War," in Brigitte L. Nacos, Robert Y. Shapiro, and Pierangelo Isernia, *Decisionmaking in a Glass House* (Lanham, MD: Rowman & Littlefield, 2000), 21.

21. *The Today Show*, NBC, March 4, 2003.

22. Mentioned in Tim Rutten, "Torture, handled lightly," *Los Angeles Times*, March 15, 2003, E1.

23. Rutten, "Torture, handled lightly."

24. Results as of September 13, 2002. See *www.e-thepeople.org* (accessed August 1, 2003).

25. *www.about.com/library/bfiles/blpoll-torturingterrorists.htm* (accessed August 1, 2003).

26. "Out of Sight, out of Mind: The Abu Ghraib story broke when we saw visual proof of torture. Why not sooner?" *Columbia Journalism Review*, July/August 2004, 6.

27. "Out of Sight, out of Mind."

28. See, for example, Ruben Navarette Jr., "Coming to terms with an unimaginable outrage," *Record* (Bergen County, NJ), May 14, 2004, L11.

29. Donald Gregg, "Fight fire with compassion," *New York Times*, June 10, 2004, 27.

30. Navarette Jr., "Coming to terms," L11.

31. For one account of Limbaugh's comments, see Anne E. Kornblut, "On Campaign Trail, Photos widen the divide on war, some say fakery, others vindication," *Boston Globe*, May 9, 2004, A11.

32. Kornblut, "On Campaign Trail."

33. Susan Sontag, "Regarding the Torture of Others," *New York Times Magazine*, May 23, 2004. Retrieved from LexisNexis April 10, 2004.

34. "The Torture Photos," *New York Times*, May 5, 2004, 26.

35. Frank Rich, "On Television, Torture takes a Holiday," *New York Times*, January 23, 2005, Arts and Leisure, 1.

36. According to surveys by the Pew Center/Princeton Survey Research Associates International, conducted June 3–13, 2004, and the Henry J. Kaiser Family Foundation/Princeton Survey Research Associates International, conducted June 4–8, 2004.

37. According to an ABC News/*Washington Post* survey conducted May 20–23, 2004.

38. ABC News/*Washington Post* survey conducted May 20–23, 2004.

39. Lelyveld, "Interrogating Ourselves," 38, 39.

40. "Torture by Proxy," *New York Times*, March 8, 2005, 22.

41. Sanford Levinson, "Brutal Logic," *Village Voice* (New York), May 18, 2004, 27.

42. Levinson, "Brutal Logic."

43. Levinson, "Brutal Logic."

44. From *Hannity & Colmes*, Fox News Network, March 5, 2003.

45. Limbaugh was quoted in Stephen Kinzer and Jim Rutenberg, "Grim images seem to deepen nation's polarization on Iraq," *New York Times*, May 13, 2004, 11.

46. The former CIA operative was introduced as Wayne Simmons when he appeared as a guest on *Hannity & Colmes* on the Fox News Network on May 13, 2004.

47. Ehud Sprinzak, "The psychological formation of extreme left terrorism in a democracy: The case of the Weathermen," in *Origins of Terrorism: Psychologies, Ideologies, Theologies, States of Mind*, ed. Walter Reich (New York: Cambridge University Press, 1990), 82.

48. Seymour Hersh, "Torture at Abu Ghraib," *New Yorker*, May 10, 2004.

49. Mark Danner, *Torture and Truth: America, Abu Ghraib, and the War on Terror* (New York: New York Review of Books, 2004), 245.

50. Adam Zagorin and Michael Duffy, "Inside the interrogation of detainee 063," *Time*, June 20, 2004, 33.

51. "Stain of Guantanamo: We do care," *New York Times*, June 22, 2004, 18.

52. "Stain of Guantanamo."

53. Jack Wheeler, "Interrogating KSM; How to make the al Qaeda terrorist sing," *Washington Times*, March 5, 2003, A19.

54. Wheeler, "Interrogating KSM."

55. *NBC Nightly News*, NBC, November 16, 2001.

56. *World News Tonight with Peter Jennings*, ABC, November 18, 2002.

57. *World News Tonight with Peter Jennings*, ABC, November 18, 2002.

58. *CNN Talkback Live*, CNN, August 15, 2002.

59. Danner, *Torture and Truth*, 227.

60. Tony Judt, "The New World Order," *New York Review of Books*, July 14, 2005, 17.

61. Judt, "The New World Order."

62. Hersh, "Torture at Abu Ghraib."

63. Hersh, "Torture at Abu Ghraib."

64. Cheney was quoted in Brian Knowlton, "Cheney backs handling of detainees at Cuba base," *Washington Post*, May 31, 2005.

65. General Massu was quoted in Michael T. Kaufman, "Jacques Massu, 94, General who led Battle of Algiers," *New York Times*, October 31, 2002, 25.

66. Kaufman, "Jacques Massu, 94."

67. Kaufman, "Jacques Massu, 94."

6

American Muslims' Sentiments in the Post-9/11 Years

Most Muslim-Americans believe that the news media's portrayal of Muslims and their religion is unfair, negative, stereotypical, and not at all reflective of the true nature of Islam and the vast majority of its followers. "The media portrays us like all Muslims are like these fanatics and we go along with bombs in our hand, pockets, and stuff like that," said one Muslim American man during a focus group session in the spring of 2003.[1] A Muslim woman agreed. "Some of the news are [sic] shameless. . . . It's beyond anything that—it's very scary actually," she said. "It's very, very scary thinking how much they can manipulate the general American population. Some of those [news organizations] are a lot worse than the others, but they're all in general bad."[2] Speaking of non-Muslim Americans, a Muslim New Yorker with roots in the Caribbean complained, "I think they see all of us as terrorists because of the media. You look at CNN. You look at Channel 5. You look at Channel 9. I mean, the only good program you can look at is Channel 13—*Frontline*."[3]

When asked by pollsters in November and December 2001, just a few months after the events of 9/11, about their views of the news media, two-thirds of Muslim Americans characterized the mainstream media as not fair in their portrayal of Muslims and Islam. Nearly two years later, three-fourths of American Muslims considered the news media to be unfair in this respect, while just as many (77 percent) considered Hollywood entertainment as unfair to Muslims and their religion. This negative perception of both news and entertainment media was shared by American Muslims regardless of their party identification and their ideological traits. African American Muslims, however, were significantly more convinced of media bias than other ethnic and racial groups within the American Muslim community in that 88 percent perceived the mainstream media and 91 percent Hollywood specifically as unfair toward Islam and Muslims.[4] Twenty-five focus group sessions conducted in the spring and summer of 2003 with Muslim American males and females of different age groups and different religious, ethnic, and professional backgrounds affirmed in far more detail than the cited poll results the extent of this deep-seated distrust of the U.S. news and entertainment media.[5] As a teenage girl put it, "You don't see them [the media] saying good things about Muslims 24-7, and then, if we ever did say anything wrong, oh, it would be on ABC, NBC—every single channel. Over and over again, they'll keep repeating to make sure that everyone out there heard the [news]—how we are."[6] A female college student objected to the media's "bashing of Islam," and an Arab American man remarked bitterly that "the media lies so much that it's not even funny."[7]

The following excerpts from a focus group session with members of the Muslim American business community in New York were representative of the expressed dissatisfaction with the way Arabs and Muslims were depicted in the news after the terrorist strikes of 9/11:

Male Voice: I mean, the unfortunate thing is—is, after the September 11, we, as a Muslim and Arab community, we tend to take the defensive posture for something that we haven't done anything, had nothing to do with.

Male Voice: Yeah, but it's the media.

Male Voice: But—yeah, I'm coming to that—But, of course, the picture that has been given about the Muslims and the Arabs is—of course, in the media, you— they are made out to be monsters. Not—and camel herders, and nothing else. I mean, every picture that they bring you, they don't even bring you a decent place or a decent street to see. They bring you just stone-throwing kids and people behind jackasses. Just to show that, "These are the Arabs, you know?" This is the— Look, they don't give you anything that is of value of the Arabs, or the Muslims.

Male Voice: America always needs a bogeyman, and we just happen to be this century's bogeyman, that's all.

Male Voice: Yeah.

Male Voice: Whether it be the Communists, or—

Male Voice: When it's finished, another one—we have to find another one.[8]

Muslim Americans resent that the news media report "all the time" about "Muslim terrorists" but not at all about "Christian terrorists." In this context, one American Muslim of South Asian descent pointed to the different terminology used to report on the long-lasting violent conflict between Catholics and Protestants in Northern Ireland:

No one has said, "Hey, the terrorists are Protestant," or even "a Christian is a terrorist." They go as IRA, XYZ. . . . But then why is it that every Muslim organization, you're known as a Muslim terrorist. It is not that, "Hey, he's part of Al Qaeda." But no, "He's a Muslim extremist, a Muslim terrorist." It's the media, which has all this [*sic*] image, which again translate in the average guy on the read. He opens the *New York Times* and he reads about all these terrorists. And then he says, "Oh, all Muslims are in the same ism boat."[9]

Muslim members of New York Police and Fire Departments were particularly vehement in charging the news media with stereotyping all Muslims as terrorists. Speaking of the "messy media" rather than the mass media, focus group members said the following:

Male Voice: And when they [the media] didn't have anything to report, then they come to the Muslim community.

Male Voice: And it seems that every—it's a license now to come after Islam because anything connected to Islam is terrorist—

Male Voice: Sorry, I don't mean to interrupt you, but that's a good point. I mean, it strikes me that when there is a terrorist and he claims to be a Muslim, then it's a Muslim terrorist. And then when there is a terrorist who is not a Muslim, it's not a Christian terrorist, it's not a Jewish terrorist.

Male voice: Right.

Male voice: It's a terrorist.

Female Voice: Yeah.

Male Voice: Why we can't, we—and why can't they just give that terrorist is a terrorist, regardless of who you are, whether you're a Muslim or not. Terrorists just be labeled as terrorists.

Moderator: That's a . . .

Male Voice: You don't have to—to, you know, to add that "Muslim" terrorist. I mean, it could be anything.[10]

While making the point that anti-Muslim stereotypes were present in the media before the events of 9/11, one woman felt that ever since, the negative portrayal "perpetuates more hate" and that as a result in the American public's mind "there's no denying that Muslims are always terrorists and no matter—and using Muslims always when talking about terrorism."[11]

A young American Muslim woman who had quit her job at one of the cable networks [not Fox News] found "the environment and the coverage that we were providing to be absolutely intolerable." In particular, she gave the following reasons for leaving this position:

[I]t was bad before, but I didn't really have any stake in it before, in terms of, you know, prejudice and bias and lack of understanding of, you know, foreign affairs and that kind of thing. But after September 11th, I mean, eighty percent of the people in the newsroom were very openly anti-Muslim and anti-Arab. . . .

And—you know, they had no kind of understanding at all of the, you know, deeper political issues that were going on. We had—the day that Baghdad fell, we had pizza and the newsroom celebrated.[12]

After she talked about the reasons for quitting the job during a focus group session, a fellow Muslim asked why she hadn't stayed on the job, tried to change the system from within, and provide another point of view. He said that American Muslims need to think strategically of ways to influence people and make "the Muslim story more mainstream."[13] This man's idea of working within the mainstream media system was not limited to the news media but to entertainment as well. He spoke of comedy shows and movies in which the Jew and the Christian and the Indian appear next to each other—but never the Muslim. "And part of it is because we didn't push our case in—in their face all the time," he concluded.

Focus group participants identified two reasons in particular as causes for what they perceive as anti-Muslim, anti-Islam, anti-Arab, anti-Palestinian, and pro-Jewish and pro-Israeli biases in American television and in print news: government and corporate influence, or Jewish and Zionist dominance in the media, or both. According to one female professional, while the media in the United States are technically not under the control of the government, there are strong ties and interrelationships. In the words of a woman lawyer, the media are "never going to portray anything other than what Washington tells them to do, because they're all in cahoots, really."[14] Another female Muslim New Yorker, who said she could not tolerate CNN and had stopped watching this network altogether, called CNN "the mouthpiece of the [U.S.] government."[15] Muslim converts were the most critical voices when it came to the American media. While one woman felt the U.S. media didn't try to tell the truth, another female Muslim charged that the American press is an "organ of the government, at this point. In times of war, they have clearance to shut everything down and they—they have."[16] Even when recognizing that a media organization had improved its coverage of Muslims, American Muslims remained suspicious and wondered about the political or governmental motives behind such a change, as the following focus group discussion revealed:

Female Voice: And I think, yes, since September 11th, because Islam has been a large focus in the States, it's been skewed and biased. But I've—I've actually noticed a difference recently, to a certain extent. I think, the *New York Times*, which has always been very biased against Islam is probably a little less so. Like, I've noticed some positive articles, which really shocked me. But, I mean, that's my impression.

Female Voice: Yeah. I—You know, I've been very cautious about it, even when it gets pro-Islam right now. My caution—I feel like, they have to—they want to set up an Iraqi government. They have to get a bit more positive now. You know?

So, I think the media—I think it's a kind of brainwashing in many ways. I really feel more—I mean, I've always thought about, you know, corporations and money and media and information. You know, and I know they do it with it—do it with advertising, in Coke, and I just feel we've taken it now to another level. You know, from Hollywood to creating emotions, they've done the same thing with—with real news. So I—you know, it's just—it's been mind-boggling to me how successfully.[17]

Later on during this exchange, one participant talked about "subtle connections" that are being made in the media between Islam and terrorism.

An imam pointed fingers at the dominance of big business in the media and mentioned a ruling by the Federal Communications Commission (FCC) designed to allow big corporations to acquire even more broadcast stations and own both broadcast and print media in one market. According to the imam, "There is no free press. Whoever controls the media controls the mind of the public, you know?"[18] The idea of the American media having lost their freedom and independence was echoed by a Muslim intellectual who spoke of a media monopoly in the hands of no more than three or four big corporations that "control TV, radio, cable, newsprint, so it's becoming difficult to engage a Muslim community—to engage the media with much success."[19] In a focus group discussion, women professionals, too, mentioned proposed FCC rulings in favor of cross-ownership in the same media markets and predicted that media tycoon Rupert Murdoch would probably buy more newspapers, more radio stations, and more TV channels.

As the following focus group exchange between the session's moderator and a Muslim American businessman showed, Zionism and Jewish influence inside the media were also cited as the reasons for anti-Muslim and anti-Arab media bias:

Moderator: Do you think that the media deliberately depicts Muslims negatively?

Male Voice: Yes, I do.

Moderator: What are—what's behind that? What's the agenda? I mean—

Male Voice: What's behind that? To start with, Zionism. Zionism is—it plays a big, big part of everything. And the government doesn't stand against that, doesn't condemn it, doesn't say anything about it. And you have people who are anti-Muslim, basically, who are being paid millions of dollars just to—to put down the Muslims in every which way they can. And this is happening on a daily basis. Continuously, just like the Coke commercials. Keep repeating the "Coke Coke Coke" until it sits in the mind, and this what—what they repeat. The in and the out. And every news station, they repeat the same thing, so—so what remains in the people's minds, who are not political to start with and very easy to convince to be against the Muslims. So once you keep hammering and hammering and hammering, that stays in the mind.

Moderator: And the message is?

Male Voice: And the message is, you know, the Arabs basically, are non—they are not part of this country. They are not part of this society. They are—they don't deserve to be part of this society. And also, by reflecting the bad images— Look, they show us to be terrorists—and—and—persona non grata for this country. So, that will continue until the American people wake up and realize what is going on in the media.[20]

A professional woman, who said that she is listening to National Public Radio (NPR) a lot and that it is by and large okay, nevertheless felt that "NPR is a Jewish station" and "the number of things that you hear cele- brating Jewish culture on NPR is just unbelievable."[21] As for the local New York Fox station, one focus group participant felt that "anything Jewish is— is phenomenal. Is fabulous . . . [and] "anything that affects Israel is por- trayed in a particular light, whereas the same exact thing might happen to a Palestinian and it's portrayed completely differently."[22]

After blaming Hollywood's motion picture industry for stereotyping Arabs and Muslims in the past and to this day, one imam charged that the *New York Times*, the *Washington Post*, the *Los Angeles Times*, the *Chicago Tri- bune*, the *Boston Globe*, and all the other major news media are "anti-Mus- lim." More specifically, the imam said with respect to the media,

When you come to Muslims and Arabs? I mean, the question—that's why every political here [*sic*] is based on the side of Zionism. Because even the average Joe six-pack thinks all Arabs got horns. Yes. All Muslims have horns. This is sad. A beautiful country like this, you know. And this image problem we have, seri- ous image problem in this country.[23]

The conviction that the media have tremendous influence on public sen- timents lies at the heart of Muslim Americans' attention to what they per- ceive as media bias. Many members of this minority believe that the news "brainwashes" the American people to embrace the media's stereotypical depiction of Muslims as fundamentally bad people. As one young Muslim girl described her feelings,

And in a way, I blame the media for the ignorance of the people, because they sit there and they make Muslims seem as if they are bad people, that they are terrorists. They're aggressive, you know, they don't think. They just—they just do whatever they want. You know, they have no morals, they have no values. And, like, the media plays a big role in [this], like, show—like, showing people, like, how we are. And they always—they always show us that we are negative.[24]

BAD NEWS, GOOD NEWS, AND THE SEARCH FOR THE TRUTH

Muslim Americans from all walks of life who participated in a series of focus groups distinguished clearly between what they perceived as biased coverage on the one hand and fair news on the other. Fox News was most often mentioned as a gross example of a U.S. media organization strongly biased against Muslims, Arabs, and Islam, with CNN, ABC News, and NBC News following right behind. On the other hand, the British Broadcasting Company (BBC) and the Canadian Broadcasting Company (CBC) were mentioned most often as the most trusted Western TV networks. Even many of those who accused the *New York Times* of reflecting an anti-Muslim slant revealed that they read the newspaper of record regularly—according to one participant, however, never the editorial and op-ed pages. Some Muslim Americans mentioned the *Wall Street Journal,* the *Economist,* and the *Guardian* as regular news sources. When one focus group participant mentioned the *Christian Science Monitor* favorably, others seemed to agree. There was praise for the Public Broadcasting System's TV programs, especially *Frontline,* as well as for National Public Radio and WBAI radio in New York City. One female college student said she used her satellite dish to watch Euro News after finding the network by accident when she was channel surfing. She praised Euro News for its balanced coverage and gave as an example that the European news network had explained the positions of both the American and Iraqi sides during the 2003 invasion of Iraq.[25]

A number of participants revealed that they themselves and many other Muslims in the United States watch Arab satellite television networks regularly, specifically Al-Jazeera and Al Manar. While nobody mentioned that Al Manar is owned by the Lebanese Hezbollah, an organization that for many years has perpetrated terrorism against Americans, other Westerners, and Israelis, one businessman said that he watches the channel and found its programs excellent. Others reported that magazine articles are "passed to you by colleagues and other people."[26]

But several participants in different focus groups were as weary of Arab and Muslim news sources as they were of the mainstream American media. When asked by the moderator about their news sources, Muslim businessmen engaged in the following discourse:

Male Voice: I'll tell you, the people I deal with most of the time, we watch every news channel that is available, including FOX, and we all have satellite stations that we watch back home, in our own languages. I watch BBC, CBC. I watch the Arab stations. And whatever talking heads tell me, the truth is somewhere in the middle. Whether they be in Arabic, from my own country, or any of the others. But I don't believe a single source. I like to take in all the sources and then make my own decision on it. And my own mind.

Male Voice: Yes—that's—that's the best.

Male Voice: That's the best way of doing it. Is to have a variety, and then make up your own mind.

Male Voice: There's just no way I'm just going to watch the Yemenese [*sic*] satellite station and believe that to be true, as well.[27]

Many focus group participants were aware of the vastly different ways in which Arab and Western media report on one and the same situation. As one Muslim man observed, while American media may tell their audiences that the U.S. military conquered a city [during the Iraq invasion], if you "watch Al Jazeera, American soldiers are still outside city walls, still trying to infiltrate."[28]

A woman complained that there are no real alternatives to the leading Western news media and that nobody seems to be reporting the news "like the Associated Press" [a wire service], namely reporting the news "objectively from the field." When asked whether she was watching Arab news as an alternative, the same woman replied, "It's just another extreme view and they're very passionate in their way of expressing everything. That's very strange to me. That's very foreign to me. So I don't find it very emotional versus objective news."[29]

During a focus group session, critics of the media in general included Muslim and Arab media organizations both abroad and in the United States as well. As one woman put it,

What I don't like to see is us always portraying ourselves as poor victims. "Oh, the poor Muslims." "Oh, Muslims." You know, "Woe is us, woe is us." It just annoys me to no end when we constantly portray ourselves as victim, victim, victim. I think that we have to give ourselves a certain sense of empowerment and—just take the bull by the horns and do what we have to do. I don't like being portrayed always as the underdog. I know we are, but I don't think that you got very far by just, you know, "Woe is us. Poor us. Poor Muslims, poor Muslims." Take that energy and use it in a way that can be productive and—[30]

INFILTRATING THE MAINSTREAM MEDIA OR ESTABLISHING A UNIFIED MUSLIM MEDIA?

The idea of getting involved in the media and thereby influencing the depiction of Muslim Americans and their religion was frequently discussed by focus group participants. According to one Muslim woman, "until we infiltrate the media, until we infiltrate politics," things will not change. The same woman observed that other groups have done this but that Muslim Americans have not. She said, "We are still in the very, very beginning process of that."[31] But there was no agreement on what approach might have the best chances of changing Muslim Americans' media image. One New Yorker said that the corporate media monopoly simply would not allow Muslim communities to interact with the mainstream media in a successful way and that therefore any effort in this respect would be a waste of his time. He advocated instead using the Internet and other means of communication in order to inform and educate the public directly. "The media will not cover good stories [about us]," he argued. "But I think we can minimize the impact of the negative stereotyping of Islam and Muslims, if we actually present counter images."[32] A college student, too, expressed the belief that it was the responsibility of the Muslim community to counter media messages that have "a lot to do with discrimination and fear." He added, "We need to speak out and stand up for ourselves."[33] A woman complained about Muslim groups having "something to do with the way we are presented in the media." She was particularly critical of American Muslims "stereotyping themselves and their fellow-Muslims" by not "presenting Islam in its true diversity." According to this woman, American Muslims must counter the notion that there is only one face of Islam, that all Muslim women look the same way, that all Muslim men look alike. Her point was that there is not only one face of Islam and that this needs to be communicated to the public at large.[34] While speaking of the necessity of working with the media, the woman looked for "leaders out there who have access to the media that we don't have."

Others reported, however, that the inability to fight with Fox News and Rupert Murdoch or others in big media organizations had not prevented them from working with individual news outlets. As one lawyer described,

> I have gotten involved with my local newspaper. I've gone to meet the editor. I have written letters-to-the-editor. I have written op-ed pieces, and I have gotten involved and I am encouraging others to get involved. . . . Don't fight it at the higher level [but] the grass root level.
>
> They have advisory boards, and I am on the advisory board of our local paper. I sit—go to every month's meeting, get involved. . . . I have a whole stack of, you know, articles up there that I've written, I mean, from Kosovo, [to] labeling Islam.[35]

Another focus group participant reported that the National Council of Churches had helped to set up a meeting of Muslims with people at the *New York Times* who assured their guests that the newspaper would follow a "balanced approach on Muslim issues, Palestinian issues, things affecting it." This Muslim New Yorker felt that coverage of Islam in the *Times* was more balanced after that.[36] The idea that they have to be proactive in efforts to change the image of Islam is supported by the vast majority of American Muslims: Following the 9/11 attacks, nine of ten members of this minority felt that Muslims should be involved with the American media and educational system in order to improve the image of their religion.[37]

Even before 9/11, there were voices among Muslim Americans who felt strongly about the need for mainstream Muslim media that would transcend the many ethnic media, such as Pakistani or Bosnian or Turkish newspapers. Pointing out that indeed most of today's Muslim media in America are ethnic, one Muslim media insider said,

> I believe that in the next ten, fifteen years most of the ethnic media will be the mainstream Muslim media. . . . We do not have a media powerful enough to reach not only the American audience, but outside America as well. We need to have something of that kind, which should be competing with AP [the wire service Associated Press] and Reuters.[38]

In order to bring the fragmented American Muslim media market together, one focus group participant suggested that there was the need for a unifying umbrella organization, what he envisioned as the "Muslim Media Association." In the words of this Muslim American: "Without that we are nothing. We are separated on [*sic*] small groups.[39]

Three years later, several focus group participants said that they were looking forward to the first shows to be aired by Bridges Television, the first channel by and for American Muslims. As one woman put it, "I think that channel is just a perfect example of the fact that Muslims—I mean, American Muslims now, especially, you know, in the—in the younger generation are wizening up and are realizing that our voices cannot get heard until we—you know, until we establish those [media] roots."[40] While some Muslim Americans thought that providing alternative views and images in the Muslim media meant simply to preach to the choir, others praised especially the establishment of the Bridges TV channel, which they considered to be just as pioneering as the creation of BET (the Black Entertainment Television channel) several decades earlier. According to one American Muslim media expert, projecting American Muslims in everyday situations in sitcoms, comedy shows, and all kinds of entertainment on Bridges could eventually affect the portrayal of Muslim Americans in the non-Muslim mainstream media as well. The idea was to brand Muslim Americans in a positive way. As one discussant said, "The problem [in much of the media] is the lack of addressing the fear that is there in the U.S. society. It's a brand name problem. It's a reputation problem, and that kills businesses, kills cultures, kills—kills communities that are trying to, you know, basically break free of those kinds of things [negative perceptions]." Indeed, recognizing some changes for the better in non-Muslim media, one American Muslim initiated the following focus group exchange:

> *Male Voice:* And one of the things that happened after 9/11 is you see Muslims more and more in the media and—and even, this is—in a comic strip. There's a comic strip *For Better and For Worse.* I don't know, it's just—it's syndicated in every newspaper in the United States except for the Times which doesn't run comics. But they've—there's a recurring character now who wears a hijab—in the cartoon.
>
> *Female Voice:* Really?
>
> *Male Voice:* And it's this small comic strip, but it's being—it's kind of entering your brain, now.
>
> *Female Voice:* And it's not a caricature? It's like a—it's a valid—
>
> *Male Voce:* No, she—she's. The kids go to school, and there's a girl in the classroom and—who wears a hijab.
>
> *Female Voice:* That's amazing.
>
> *Male Voice:* So she's in the classroom, she's in the cafeteria. And she's just wearing [a] hijab.
>
> *Female Voice:* That's amazing.
>
> *Male Voice:* So it—that makes it normal.[41]

While the participants in the focus group sessions we described were particularly sophisticated and very attentive consumers of both domestic and international news, nearly three-fourths of American Muslims informed themselves daily and nearly one-fourth several times a week about international affairs. Television was the most important news source for more than half of American Muslims, 17 percent got their news mostly from the Internet, and an additional 13 percent relied chiefly on newspapers. For those who identified television as their primary source of information on foreign affairs, 38 percent mentioned CNN and 14 percent ABC News as their preferred channels, while 15 percent watched other international or domestic channels.[42] By 2004, only a quarter of American Muslims identified themselves as regular consumers of media sources that addressed themselves to ethnic groups, but three-quarters said they did not follow ethnic newspapers or other ethnic media regularly.[43]

OPINIONS ON THE "WAR ON TERRORISM" AND U.S. MIDDLE EAST POLICY

So far, this chapter has examined focus group discussions with American Muslims of different ethnic, religious, and professional backgrounds in order to get a sense of what individual members of this minority think about the mainstream media in the United States and their effects on the American public at large—especially since the events of 9/11. We also learned from these focus group participants a great deal about their views of influential non-American media and the multitude of ethnic media outlets in the United States specifically directed at Muslim audiences. In the following section, we rely on the few representative surveys of Muslim Americans—most of them U.S. citizens—that were undertaken after the events of 9/11 in late 2001, in early 2002, and in the late summer of 2004. All three of these polls were conducted by Zogby International, the two most comprehensive ones for Project MAPS: Muslims in American Public Square at Georgetown University and the third for the Hamilton College Muslim America Poll. We concentrated on those parts of these surveys that related directly or indirectly to American Muslims' major concerns in post-9/11 America and in the post-9/11 world.

When asked in late 2001, only weeks after the attacks of 9/11, for whom they had voted in the presidential election of 2000, a plurality of American Muslims (42 percent) told pollsters that they had cast their vote for George W. Bush, the Republican candidate, and 31 percent said they had voted for Al Gore, the candidate of the Democratic Party. Looking back to the weeks after 9/11, a clear majority of the Muslim minority gave President Bush high grades (27 percent excellent and 31 percent good) for handling the terrorist attacks on the World Trade Center and the Pentagon, 21 percent rated his performance as fair, and only 17 percent rated it as poor. When asked how confident they were of President Bush's ability to handle "this crisis," most American Muslims said they were very confident (29 percent) or confident (28 percent), while only a minority were either a little nervous (25 percent) or very nervous (15 percent). Indeed, during the post-9/11 weeks most members of the American Muslim minority were part of the mighty wave of patriotic unity that swept the nation in response to the terrorist attacks: 41 percent of American Muslims felt more patriotic than before 9/11, and 52 percent said that their patriotism had not changed, while only 5 percent revealed less patriotic sentiments.[44]

Nearly four years later, only weeks before the 2004 presidential election, President Bush and the Republicans had lost significant ground in the Muslim American electorate: 76 percent of the respondents said they would vote for the John Kerry/John Edwards ticket; only 7 percent intended to cast their votes for President Bush and Vice President Richard Cheney. At the time, 50 percent of Muslim voters identified themselves as Democrats and 12 percent as Republicans, compared to 40 percent Democrats and 28 percent Republicans in late 2001. The reason for this significant shift was no mystery: the majority of eligible Muslim voters said they were disappointed by President Bush and opposed to his policies and decisions in response to

9/11, particularly with respect to the war in Iraq and issues of civil liberties that touched on their lives. For 51 percent of American Muslims, "being Muslim" was a very important factor in their voting decisions, and for an additional 18 percent an important factor, while 29 percent said that their religious belief was not an important consideration. A majority felt, however, that Muslims should vote as a bloc for one of the presidential candidates in the 2004 elections.[45]

A comparison of surveys conducted in late 2001, in the spring of 2002, and in the summer of 2004 reveals a dramatic shift in American Muslims' attitudes toward U.S. counterterrorism policies abroad during these years. This was particularly the case with respect to the United States–led military actions in Afghanistan and the perceived targets of the "war on terror." When asked in late 2001 about their positions on the military actions against Afghanistan, a 51 percent majority of American Muslims supported the measures strongly (29 percent) or somewhat (22 percent), whereas 43 percent were somewhat (17 percent) or strongly (26 percent) opposed.[46] About six months later, nothing had changed in that again half of the poll respondents felt that the Afghan military actions were "justified under the circumstances," while 43 percent thought otherwise.[47] But by the late summer of 2004 the attitudes of American Muslims had drastically changed in that in hindsight 53 percent opposed the military actions against Afghanistan, while 35 percent remained supportive. At the same time, the opposition against the Iraq war was massive: 81 percent of Muslims in America opposed and only 13 percent supported the war. When asked why the United States was fighting the Iraq war, 39 percent said the reason was America's determination to control Middle Eastern oil, 16 percent mentioned the desire to dominate the region, and 16 percent were convinced that the U.S. move against Iraq was about protecting Israel.[48] As table 6.1 shows, two-thirds of American Muslims felt in late 2001, after the military measures against Afghanistan had commenced, that the United States was fighting a war against terrorism, while less than one of five felt that the true target was Islam. Six months later, in April 2002, American Muslims were less convinced that

Table 6.1. American Muslims and U.S. Post-9/11 Military Actions: From a Perceived War on Terrorism to a War on Islam

	War on Terrorism (%)	War on Islam (%)	Not Sure/Other (%)
Oct./Nov. 2001	67	18	16
April 2002	40	33	27
Aug./Sept. 2004	33	38	29

Sources: Project MAPS/Zogby and Hamilton College Muslim America Poll.

America's response to the attacks of 9/11 amounted to a war on terrorism: 40 percent still thought so, but 33 percent believed that the United States was really was making war on Islam. Weeks before the 2004 presidential elections, still more American Muslims (38 percent) were convinced that the United States was fighting a war against Islam and not involved in a war on terrorism (33 percent).

In chapter 4, we examined the American public's attitudes toward American Muslims and Muslims abroad and their religion and pointed to the large number of survey respondents who either said they had no opinion, were not sure, or refused to answer. In this context, we discussed the "spiral of silence" and the poll respondents' desire to appear politically correct as an explanation for the reluctance to voice opinions or give contradictory answers. At a time when they feared they might become the targets of religious and ethnic profiling, eavesdropping, and other "counterterrorist" measures, a substantial number of American Muslims, too, seemed reluctant to give clear-cut answers. Thus, when asked in the spring of 2002 about who the perpetrators of the 9/11 terrorism were, an exceptionally large number of respondents (44 percent) either refused to answer or said they were not sure; 34 percent said that Al Qaeda and bin Laden were responsible, and 22 percent believed that some other group had struck.[49]

Several weeks after the United States–led coalition began military actions against Al Qaeda members and their Taliban friends in Afghanistan, a slight majority of American Muslims expressed support for this move, but at the same time nearly two-thirds believed that this response could result in more anti-American terrorism. More than two years later, three in four American Muslims (78 percent) believed that the Iraq war could lead to more terrorism against the United States. But whether the focus was on Afghanistan or Iraq, when asked to choose one way to fight the war on terrorism, a vast majority of American Muslims (67 percent in late 2001 and 76 percent in August/September 2004) opted for "changing America's Middle East policy." This was hardly a surprising top pick by a group in which more than 60 percent believed that there was a connection between the 9/11 attacks and U.S. policy in the Middle East. Probably based on this conviction, three in five American Muslims thought that the terrorist attacks on the World Trade Center could have been prevented, while less than two in five felt that the strikes were unavoidable.[50]

Moreover, as table 6.2 shows, a large majority of American Muslims were consistent in overwhelmingly advocating U.S. support for Palestinian statehood, a reduction in U.S. financial aid to Israel, and less support for undemocratic regimes in the Middle East.

Table 6.2.   American Muslims and U.S. Foreign Policy in the Middle East

	Nov./Dec. 2002 (%)	Aug./Sept. 2004 (%)
U.S. should support Palestinian state	84	87
U.S. should reduce financial aid to Israel	70	80
U.S. should reduce support for undemocratic regimes in the Muslim world	61	66

Sources: MAPS/Zogby 2001 and MAPS/Zogby 2004

AMERICAN MUSLIMS AND THE POST-9/11 DOMESTIC CONTEXT

Several weeks after the attacks in New York and Washington, 59 percent of American Muslims were very satisfied (20 percent) or somewhat satisfied (39 percent) with how things were going in America at the time, while 25 percent were somewhat dissatisfied and 12 percent very dissatisfied. But nearly three years later, in the late summer of 2004, 63 percent of Muslims in America, and thus a very solid majority, were very dissatisfied (32 percent) or somewhat dissatisfied (31 percent), compared to merely 35 percent who were very satisfied (7 percent) or somewhat satisfied (28 percent). Yet, even as their dissatisfaction with the status quo and trends in American society grew rapidly, 51 percent felt nevertheless that it was still a good time "to be a Muslim in America," whereas 36 percent said it was a bad time and 13 percent were not sure.[51] While American Muslims were certainly aware of and uneasy about foreign policy issues, domestic policy was of even greater concern for them in the post-9/11 years. Thus, when asked before the 2004 presidential election about the most important factor that would affect their voting decision, 44 percent picked domestic policy and 34 percent foreign policy. This primary concern with domestic politics and policies was confirmed when respondents were asked to list the most important issue facing the Muslim American community. In late 2001, the three most often named issues were (1) stereotyping, prejudice, profiling, and racism (20 percent); (2) American and Muslim relations and images (15 percent); and (3) ignorance, misunderstanding, discrimination (12 percent). More than two years later, respondents named (1) constitutional issues (28 percent); (2) bias and racism (24 percent); and (3) becoming mainstream (11 percent). While in late 2001 foreign policy was mentioned by only 1 percent of respondents, it was picked by 10 percent nearly three years later and moved into fourth place on the list of the most important issues facing the Muslim American minority.[52] But the most obvious change in the nearly two years separating these two surveys was the growing concern among American Muslims that their civil liberties were being curbed and that they faced discrimination by and separation from mainstream America. In April 2002, 27 percent of American Muslims said that they had personally experienced anti-Muslim discrimination, harassment, verbal abuse, or physical attack since 9/11 and 53 percent knew of Muslims in their area who had suffered this sort of abuse. But at the same time, 70 percent revealed that non-Muslim fellow Americans had expressed their support during the post-9/11 period.[53] When surveyed in August and September 2004, respondents revealed higher rates of anti-Muslim mistreatment in that 40 percent said that they themselves had suffered from such discrimination and 57 percent knew of friends or family members being discriminated against because of their religion. At the same time, 26 percent of respondents said that they themselves had been subject to profiling. When asked in what setting respondents themselves, friends, or family members had experienced anti-Muslim discrimination, 32 percent mentioned specifically the place of work, 27 percent the company of friends, acquaintances, and neighbors, and 21 percent school. Those who knew firsthand of anti-Muslim discrimination mentioned first verbal abuses, followed by racial profiling by police resulting in being stopped, searches, arrests, destruction of property, denial of employment, physical abuse, and boycotting of Muslim- or Arab-operated businesses.[54]

Although opposed to counterterrorist measures that specifically target and discriminate against Muslim and Arab Americans and Muslim and Arab noncitizens as well, the vast majority in this minority had in many respects the same security concerns as non-Muslim Americans. It is interesting to note here that the overall American public agreed that Muslim Americans were the particular targets of counterterrorist measures. When asked whether the provisions of the Patriot Act would be used to investigate Muslim Americans, nearly half of the U.S. public felt this to be extremely or very likely and an additional third "somewhat likely."[55] Yet, surprisingly, even three years after 9/11 and thus after a period in which many of them had been affected by the implementation of counterterrorist laws, more than two-thirds of American Muslims (69 percent) were still in favor of "stronger laws to fight terrorism."[56]

Moreover, the majority of American Muslims told pollsters several weeks after 9/11 and again nearly three years after the attacks that in their own experience and overall, Americans had been respectful and tolerant of Muslims. However, as table 6.3 shows, about half of those who commented positively on individual Americans in this respect felt at the same time that American society overall is disrespectful and intolerant of Muslims. In the

Table 6.3.   American Muslims, Individual Americans, and U.S. Society

	Nov./Dec.2001 (%)	*Aug./Sept.2004* (%)
In my experience and overall, Americans have been respectful and tolerant of Muslims	41	32
In my experience, Americans have been respectful and tolerant of Muslims, but American society overall is disrespectful and intolerant of Muslims	33	35
In my experience and overall, Americans have been disrespectful and intolerant of Muslims	8	12
In my experience, Americans have been disrespectful and intolerant of Muslims, but American society overall is respectful and tolerant of Muslims	13	16
Not Sure	4	5

Source: MAPS/Zogby 2001 and 2004

nearly three-year period between the two surveys, there was a 7 point decrease in the number of Muslims who felt that Americans as individuals were tolerant and respectful of Muslims and a 7 point increase in those who felt that individual Americans had been disrespectful and intolerant of Muslims. While it was reassuring that three years after 9/11 two-thirds of Muslims in the United States considered non-Muslims to be tolerant and respectful toward them, it was disconcerting that nearly three in ten American Muslims characterized non-Muslim Americans as intolerant and disrespectful based on their own experiences and their overall knowledge about American society.

And yet, when violent protests erupted in the Muslim world and demonstrators threatened violence and terrorism in the United Kingdom and elsewhere in the West in response to the gross depiction of the Prophet Muhammad in political cartoons first published in Denmark and thereafter in other European countries, the United States remained mostly untouched by this controversy. With few exceptions, American news organizations did not publicize the offensive caricatures that showed the Prophet Muhammad and by extension Islam as the causes of terrorism. While many in the West perceived these drawings as merely insensitive, Muslims rejected them as blasphemy and an insult to their religion. To the extent that American Muslims reacted to the original publication of the caricatures and reprints in a few U.S. publications, they did so in perfectly legitimate ways by holding news conferences, issuing statements, writing letters-to-the-editor, contacting media organizations, organizing peaceful demonstrations, and calling and actually planning for meetings of Muslim and non-Muslim Americans to promote better mutual understanding of their religions. Here democracy worked as it should.

The different reactions by Muslims in Western Europe and in the United States were indicative of the differences between American Muslims and their brethren in Denmark and France, the United Kingdom and the Netherlands, Germany and Belgium, and other European countries. The mass of Muslims and Arabs in Europe live separate and unequal lives, often in slumlike conditions, and are alienated from the cultural, religious, social, and political values of the non-Muslim majority. They are frustrated and angry and are seen and treated like alien threats by indigenous populations. Given this situation, it has been increasingly difficult for voices of reason to be heard on either side. In comparison to the Muslim diaspora in Europe, American Muslims and Arabs are far more part of their country's mainstream and actually rank above the national average in terms of educational level and socioeconomic status.

To be sure, all is not well in this country either—far from it—as we have described in this book. But given the vastly different situations of Muslims here and abroad that also help to explain the different reactions to the cartoon controversy, we end on an optimistic note. For if there is hope for bridging the gap between different religious and ethnic values and traditions, the prospect seems far better in this nation of immigrants from all over the globe than in the traditionally homogenous societies of Europe.

NOTES

1. From a focus group session with Muslims of South Asian background on April 23, 2003.

2. From a focus group session with Muslims of South Asian background on April 23, 2003.

3. From a focus group session with Muslims of Caribbean descent conducted on May 29, 2003.

4. According to surveys conducted for Project MAPS (Muslims in American Public Square) at Georgetown University by Zogby International in November 2001 and August/September 2004. These surveys will be referenced henceforth as MAPS/Zogby 2001 and MAPS/Zogby 2004.

5. All of the focus groups sessions mentioned in this chapter were conducted within the Muslim Communities in New York project at Columbia University in the spring and summer of 2003.

6. The remarks were made during a focus group session with a female Muslim teenager on May 18, 2003.

7. These remarks were made a during focus group session with Muslim female college students on April 21, 2003, and with Arab American Muslims on April 28, 2003.

8. From a focus group session with Muslim businessmen on May 5, 2003.

9. This opinion was voiced by a New York Muslim of South Asian descent during a focus group discussion on April 23, 2003.

10. From the transcript of a focus group session with Muslim members of the New York City Police and Fire Departments conducted on July 21, 2003.

11. These remarks were made during a focus group discussion with American Muslims from the Balkans in June 2003.

12. From a focus group session with American Muslims in the media on June 11, 2003.

13. From a focus group session with American Muslims in the media on June 11, 2003.

14. The remark was made by a Muslim of South Asian descent during a focus group session on April 23, 2003.

15. The remark was made during a focus group discussion with Sufis on June 2, 2003.

16. From a focus group discussion with Americans who converted to Islam on June 16, 2003.

17. From a focus group exchange between Muslims working in the health field on May 7, 2003.

18. From a focus group discussion with imams on June 4, 2003.

19. From a focus group discussion with Muslim intellectuals on June 9, 2003.

20. From a focus group session with Muslim businessmen on May 5, 2003.

21. This remark was made during a focus group session with professional Muslim women held on June 21, 2003.

22. Focus group session with professional Muslim women on June 21, 2003

23. The imam made these remarks during a focus group discussion on June 4, 2003.

24. Remark by a female Muslim high school student during a focus group discussion on May 18, 2003.

25. From a focus group discussion with female Muslim college students on April 21, 2003.

26. From a focus group session with Muslim businessmen on May 5, 2005.

27. From a focus group session with Muslim businessmen on May 5, 2005.

28. The comment was made by a Muslim Arab American during a focus group session on April 28, 2005.

29. From a focus group session with Muslim Americans from the Balkans in June 2003.

30. From a focus group session with Muslims working in the New York City Fire and Police Departments on July 21, 2003.

31. These remarks were made during a focus group session with Muslims working in the medical field on May 7, 2003.

32. This remark was made during a focus group session with American Muslim intellectuals on June 9, 2003.

33. The young Muslim American made these comments during a focus group session with male Muslim college students on April 17, 2003.

34. The remarks were made by a female Muslim activist during a focus group session on April 14, 2003.

35. These remarks were made during a focus group session with Muslims working in the legal field on June 9, 2003.

36. From a focus group session with Muslims working in the legal field, June 9, 2003.

37. MAPS/Zogby 2001.

38. The remarks were made on July 29, 2000, during a focus group discussion with Muslim Americans working in the media.

39. From a focus group discussion with Muslim Americans working in the media on July 29, 2000.

40. The comment was made during a focus group session on May 7, 2003, with Muslim Americans working in the medical field.

41. From a focus group session on 2003 with American Muslims in the media field.

42. MAPS/Zogby 2004, *www.projectmaps.com* (accessed December 27, 2005).

43. MAPS/Zogby 2004, *www.projectmaps.com* (accessed December 27, 2005).

44. MAPS/Zogby 2001, 16, 17.

45. MAPS/Zogby 2001 and MAPS/Zogby 2004.

46. MAPS/Zogby 2001.

47. The Hamilton College Muslim America Poll, funded by Hamilton College's Arthur Levitt Public Affairs Center, was conducted in April 2002 by Zogby International.

48. MAPS/Zogby 2004.

49. Hamilton College Muslim America Poll.

50. MAPS/Zogby 2001 and 2004.

51. MAPS/Zogby 2001 and 2004.

52. MAPS/Zogby 2001 and 2004.

53. Hamilton College Muslim America Poll.

54. MAPS/Zogby 2004.

55. Center for Survey Research and Analysis, University of Connecticut, survey conducted August 4–22, 2005.

56. Center for Survey Research and Analysis, University of Connecticut, survey conducted August 4–22, 2005.

Epilogue: Covering American Muslims and Islam

"Fear and apprehension of racial unrest and violence are deeply rooted in American society," concluded the Kerner Commission in its analysis of the urban riots of the 1960s.[1] Fear and apprehension of terrorism and violence by Muslims and Arabs are part of the American psyche since the attacks of September 11, 2001. The Kerner Report did not charge that the media caused the devastating inner city riots in Detroit and other cities but pointed out that the news coverage affected the public's attitudes toward these violent events and toward Black Americans. In one of its multiple recommendations, the commission urged the news media to open their lily-white newsrooms to African Americans with the expectation that this would lead to a more representative coverage of the black minority. In the commission's words, "to be complete, the coverage must be representative. We suggest that the main failure of the media last summer [in their reporting of the most lethal riot in Detroit in 1967] was that the totality of its coverage was not as representative as it should have been to be accurate."[2]

Given the international character of the 9/11 attacks, the 9/11 Commission was understandably not concerned with the media's reporting on Muslim and Arab Americans. But the similarities in the coverage of Black Americans in general and the violent outbursts in inner city slums in particular several decades ago and that of Muslim and Arab Americans in our times are inescapable. As described in the preceding chapters, just as the news about black Americans was far from coming close to reality, the typical coverage of Muslim and Arab Americans before and after 9/11 did not provide readers, listeners, and viewers with a representative picture of these minorities either. In addition, the mostly one-sided coverage of Muslims and Arabs overseas left its marks on Americans' perceptions of these minorities inside the United States. While newsrooms are still far from reflecting the demographic realities of the American populace, the number of African Americans in the news media has more than doubled since the Kerner Commission made its recommendations, and this may have something to do with the disappearance of outright anti-black bias in the news media. Similarly, one would expect more inclusive reporting on Muslim and Arab Americans if members of these groups had input in decisions on what news is reported and how. One year after the attacks of 9/11 Sandra Ali, an Arab and Muslim American reporter and anchor at a television station in Detroit, concluded that coverage at her particular station improved because Arab and Muslim Americans helped staffers to understand the diversity within these groups and why they should not use the term "Islamic terrorist."[3] For this reason, Sandra Ali, who has become "the newsroom expert on issues related to Arab Americans and Muslims," would prefer more Arab and Muslim Americans in mainstream newsrooms for the sake of "more accurate stories."[4] One way to strive for a more complete picture of Muslims and Arabs in the news would be, for example, not to focus only on the most extreme fringes but to also seek out moderate voices.

In 1968, the Kerner Commission made perfectly clear that freedom of the press was not the issue in its critique of the media and that "only a press unhindered by government can contribute to freedom."[5] Today, freedom of the press is not and must not be made the issue when it comes to pointing out flaws in the mass-mediated portrayal of Muslim Americans and, by extension, of Muslims in general and of their religion. The point was then and is now that a free press should make responsible decisions and choices all the time and thus also in reporting about ethnic, racial, religious, and other groups. As the American Society of Newspaper Editors puts it in the preamble of its ethics rules, "The First Amendment, protecting freedom of expression from abridgment by any law, guarantees to the people through their press a constitutional right and thereby places on newspaper people a particular responsibility."[6]

The reactions to the notorious Danish cartoons in the Western and in the Muslim worlds demonstrated that different concepts of press freedom and press responsibility result in vastly different understandings. Religious and political Muslim leaders—and eventually their followers—directed their protests to Western government officials, first in Denmark, later in other European countries where newspapers had reprinted the images of the Prophet Muhammad. They asked that governments punish harshly the cartoonists and the editors responsible for publishing the material. Given that in Muslim countries press freedom must be exercised in accordance with religious laws and traditions and morals, it was not entirely surprising that Muslim leaders pressed governments in the West to punish the "offenders." It was just as expected that European governments refused by pointing to their principle of noninterference in press freedom unless specific laws are violated.

Of course, it was an entirely different issue whether the *Jutland Post* was responsible in enlisting and publishing the controversial cartoons and whether a number of newspapers in Europe and a very few in the United States discharged their responsibility when they decided in favor of republishing the original images. William J. Bennett, a conservative, and Alan M. Dershowitz, a liberal, criticized the American mainstream media for failing to discharge their responsibility by not publicizing the cartoons. In an op-ed article in the *Washington Post*, they wrote:

> To put it simply, radical Islamists have won a war of intimidation. They have cowed the major news media from showing these cartoons. The mainstream press has capitulated to the Islamists—their threats more than their sensibilities. One did not see Catholics claiming the right to mayhem in the wake of the republished depiction of the Virgin Mary covered in cow dung, any more than one saw a rejuvenated Jewish Defense League take to the street or blow up an office when Ariel Sharon was depicted as Hitler or when the Israeli Army was depicted as murdering the baby Jesus.[7]

For Bennett and Dershowitz the news media had violated the fundamental meaning of the First Amendment's grant of press freedom, namely, that "without responsibility for the right to know carried out by courageous writers, editors, political cartoonists, and publishers, our democracy would be weaker, if not nonexistent. There should be no group or mob veto of a story that is in the public interest."[8]

Indeed, violence, threats of violence, and boycotts aimed at inflicting great financial harm should not affect the content of the media of a liberal democracy. In the case of the Danish cartoons, news organizations were forced to decide whether it was more important to demonstrate their commitment to press freedom in the face of violence or to refrain from republicizing offensive images that were hardly in the public interest apart from the violence they had caused already and were likely to refuel. Unlike critics like Bennett and Dershowitz, others did not find the self-restraint of most American news organizations wrong or extraordinary. As Robert Wright wrote in an op-ed article in the *New York Times*,

> Even many Americans who condemn the cartoon's publication accept the premise that the now-famous Danish newspaper editor set out to demonstrate: in the West we don't generally let interest groups intimidate us into what he called "self-censorship." What non-sense. Editors at mainstream American media outlets delete lots of words, sentences and images to avoid offending interest groups, especially ethnic and religious ones.[9]

He also pointed out, "The paper that [originally] published the Muhammad cartoon, it turns out, had earlier rejected cartoons of Christ because, as the Sunday editor explained in an e-mail to the cartoonist who submitted them, they would provoke an outcry."[10] It is indeed true that media organizations in the United States and elsewhere in the West have practiced self-censorship in anticipation of hostile reactions and in response to organized pressure groups' orchestrated protests to avoid advertising boycotts or shrinking ratings and subscriptions. The cartoon case was different in that the protests, orchestrated by religious and political leaders in several Muslim countries, escalated into lethal and destructive riots. Had the reactions to the cartoons overseas been as peaceful as in the United States, media reporting would have been far less prominent and the question of whether or not to republish the cartoons deemed less problematic.

As Justice William Brennan noted in *The New York Times Company v. Sullivan*, in a free and open society there will be both "good speech" and "bad speech." He was right in that publishers, editors, producers, and reporters have the freedom to decide for and against publicizing text and visual images that will please some and will offend others. However, responsible media personnel and organizations never should and never will publicize any material simply to insult, anger, or stereotype the members of particular groups. Whether media content is motivated by the responsibility to provide the public with important information or by malevolent intentions, the right of free speech also guarantees offended individuals and groups the right to express their opposition in various forms of peaceful actions. That is precisely what Muslim Americans did in response to the few cases in which U.S. media outlets republished some of the cartoons.

In conclusion, it is important to reiterate the following: The incomplete news portrayal of Muslim and Arab Americans (and Arabs and Muslims in general) that contributes and reinforces persistent stereotypes of these minorities can only be remedied by the media themselves, never by government interference and never by violence or threats of violence. This is understood and accepted in the American context. Had the same understanding and acceptance existed in the global context, the Danish cartoons may not have been published at all or, if they were, may not have fueled violence.

NOTES

1. Kerner Commission, *U.S. Riot Commission Report* (New York: Bantam Books, 1968), 365.

2. Kerner Commission, *U.S. Riot Commission Report*, 365.

3. Lillian R. Dunlap, "Remembering Reactions to 9/11," *Poynteronline*, September 10, 2002, www.poynter.org/content/content_print.asp?id=6695&custom (accessed March 17, 2006).

4. Dunlap, "Remembering Reactions to 9/11."

5. Dunlap, "Remembering Reactions to 9/11," 362.

6. From the American Society of Newspaper Editors' "Statement of Principles," available at the organization's web site at www.asne.org/kiosk/archive/principl.htm.

7. William J. Bennett and Alan M. Dershowitz, "A Failure of the Press," *Washington Post,* February 23, 2006, A19.

8. Bennett and Dershowitz, "A Failure of the Press," A19.

9. Robert Wright, "The Silent Treatment," *New York Times,* February 17, 2006, 23.

10. Wright, "The Silent Treatment," 23.

Appendix: Research Considerations and Methodologies

CHAPTER ONE

It was clear at the outset that the quantity of news about the Muslim and Arab minority was significantly larger after the events of September 11, 2001, than before; we therefore selected the twelve-month period preceding 9/11 and the six months thereafter for our main comparisons. By extending the duration of the preattack period, we avoided possible distortions caused by the limited number of cases in the six months before 9/11. For example, in the six months before 9/11 the *New York Post* reported about, quoted, or referred to the Nation of Islam, African American Muslims, and Black Muslims so frequently that members of these groups represented 20 percent of all sources in such stories. But this prominence in the selection of sources was not at all representative for the news that the *Post* published over a longer period of time. Still, whenever there was an opportunity to add to the understanding of the twelve-months versus six-months comparison, we contrasted the shorter pre-9/11 period with the post-9/11 period of equal length. We retrieved the articles and transcripts from the LexisNexis online archives using the search words "Muslim American" and "American Muslim," "Arab American" and "American Arab," "black Muslim," "Nation of Islam," and "Muslim convert." In many instances these search words produced the same texts several times, but the duplicates were discarded.

We kept track of the placement of articles (front pages, inside pages), the type of news (straight reporting, news analysis, editorial, column, letters-to-the-editor), the geographical context (New York City, domestic, international topics), news sources, themes or topics addressed in each news item, and positions or policy preferences expressed by or attributed to news sources. Coders also evaluated whether a news story's full content depicted American Muslims or Arabs in a positive, negative, or neutral light. (The actual coding choices were positive/supportive; probably positive/supportive; neutral/ambiguous; probably negative/critical of; negative/critical of.)

Finally, articles were categorized according to their framing modes—narrow or episodic, broader or thematic, or equally both, following a coding scheme used in an earlier research project by Shanto Iyengar. We met several times with our coders, six undergraduate and graduate students, explained and discussed the various coding categories, conducted joint practice sessions, and asked each of the students to individually code several sets of articles in order to check coding reliability. Once a satisfactory degree of intercoding reliability was established, the six students began the task of analyzing the content of all retrieved articles. In our first test coding rounds, our coders did not achieve a high degree of reliability in the coding of sources, themes or topics, and policy positions: the best intercoding correlation (gamma)was .75 for sources, .59 for themes, and .61 for policy preferences. But when we collapsed similar sources (i.e., Muslim American, South East Asian Muslim American, etc.) into larger categories, the results were far better (.92). Similarly, some of the policy preferences with respect to civil liberties issues were so specific that it was difficult for coders to make fine distinctions. When we bundled very similar positions together in our reliability tests, the correlation went up to .93. With respect to themes, coders tended to identify not simply one or two predominant themes or topics per story but half a dozen or more. When the focus was on the overriding theme of a story, the reliability was nearly perfect (.99). Because we had a very diverse group of coders in terms of ethnic and religious background, we expected that agreement between them on the depiction of Muslim and Arab Americans, Muslims and Arabs in general, and the framing modes would be very unlikely. Indeed, we asked the coders to use their initial sentiments to code these categories. Our goal here was simply to get input from the diverse group members in order to compare their subjective evaluations in the months before and after 9/11. That is precisely how readers of different backgrounds react to the news day in and day out. As it happened, in their evaluations of how Muslim and Arab Americans were depicted, the coding reliability was surprisingly high (.75), but it was very low with respect to Muslims and Arabs in general (.18) and quite low with respect to the framing modes (.35).

We coded all news items that reported on or made reference to American Muslims and Arabs regardless of whether the context was local/regional, national, or international. As long as Muslim Americans or Arab Americans were the topics of these articles or were simply cited or mentioned, we deemed the news relevant for our study. But in order to trace possible differences in the reporting patterns of local, national, and international news that referred directly to Muslim and Arab Americans, we kept track of articles in those three "geographical context" categories. Altogether, we analyzed 867 newspaper articles. We used the same methodology to examine transcripts of *The Early Show* and the *Evening News with Dan Rather*.

CHAPTER TWO

We content analyzed the four newspapers that we examined in our initial project—this time around for a one-month period from August 18, 2002, to September 18, 2002. Using the same retrieval methods as before and the same coding scheme, our anniversary data are based on a total of 128 news articles published by the *New York Times* (42 articles), the *New York Daily News* (18 articles), the *New York Post* (56 articles), and *USA Today* (12 articles). All of these news items were either exclusively about members of the Muslim and Arab minorities in the United States or at least mentioned them. Even if one considers that the coverage spiked around the first anniversary, the volume of this sort of news during the one-month period was at a level comparable to the six months after 9/11, when we found a total of 653 pertinent stories (about 109 per month), and much higher than in the pre-9/11 period, when the coverage of Muslim and Arab Americans was very infrequent (with a total of 59 relevant stories in the six months before 9/11 and a total of 214 stories in the twelve months before 9/11). In short, the sheer quantity of this kind of news remained on the very high level the weeks and months after 9/11.

During the same pre- and post-9/11 anniversary period, we taped the *CBS Evening News with Dan Rather* as well as one of the local evening broadcasts on WCBS and Fox Channel Five. While the CBS network news program contained a total of 70 segments that were about Muslim and/or Arab Americans or at least mentioned these minorities, we recorded 19 pertinent segments in the local news of Fox Channel Five and only four on WCBS, CBS's local affiliate in the New York metropolitan area.

CHAPTER THREE

The examination of photographic images in the weekly newsmagazines *Time* and *Newsweek* was of particular interest because we were able to get hold of the actual issues of these publications for the six months before 9/11 in addition to those covering the six-month period thereafter. This allowed us to conduct systematic quantitative and qualitative content analyses of visuals that were sharper and of an altogether better print quality than the pictures in magazine issues available on microfilm or microfiche. Relevant

130 *Appendix*

pictures that were published in the *New York Times*, the *New York Daily News*, the *New York Post*, and *USA Today* in the six months after 9/11 were also part of our quantitative analysis; we did not have hardcopies of these publications for the pre-9/11 period and decided that the images on microfilm or microfiche were not suited for our purposes. But we also examined the visuals in the four daily newspapers for several weeks before and after the first anniversary of 9/11 in order to find out whether the selection of pictures was similar to or different from that in the weeks and months following the attacks on New York and Washington.

Our first objective was simply to establish how many photographs that depicted Arabs and Muslims in New York, the United States, and abroad were published by the various news organizations we looked at. Our coders distinguished between Muslims and Arabs depicted in the context of the New York metropolitan area, across the United States, and overseas. In many instances it was not clear from viewing the pictures and the captions whether members of these ethnic and religious groups in the metropolitan New York or the U.S. domestic context were citizens, legal residents, illegal immigrants, foreign nationals with temporary visas, or had some other status. Second, coders evaluated whether the visuals portrayed members of these groups in positive, probably positive, neutral/ambiguous, probably negative, or negative ways.

But by counting the number of pictures and recording whether coders perceived images as positive or negative, one doesn't capture the rich details of visuals. The most important part of our research here was probably the interpretive analysis of relevant photographs in *Time* and *Newsweek* in the six months before and after 9/11 and around the first 9/11 anniversary.

Next, we examined randomly selected television news programs available to viewers in the New York metropolitan area—one of the network evening newscasts (*CBS News with Dan Rather*) and the evening newscasts of two local stations (WCBS Channel 2 and WNYW Fox Channel 5). We began our tapings in October 2001, several weeks after 9/11, and continued through December 2001. Finally, we also taped and examined news broadcasts in the weeks before and after the first anniversary of 9/11.

Selected Bibliography

Altheide, David L. "Three-in-one News: Network Coverage of Iran." *Journalism Quarterly* 59 (Fall 1982): 482–86.

Bennett, W. Lance. "An Introduction to Journalism Norms and Representations of Politics." *Political Communication* 13, no. 4 (1996): 103–25.

Campbell, Christopher P. *Race, Myth, and the News*. Thousand Oaks, CA: Sage, 1995.

Danner, Mark. *Torture and Truth: America, Abu Ghraib, and the War on Terror*. New York: New York Review of Books, 2004.

Dauber, Cori E. "The Shots seen 'round the World: The Impact of the Images of Mogadishu on American Military Operations." *Rhetoric and Public Affairs* 4, no. 4 (2001): 653–87.

Dershowitz, Alan M. *Why Terrorism Works: Understanding the Threat, Responding to the Challenge*. New Haven: Yale University Press, 2002.

Entman, Robert M. "Declaration of Independence: The Growth of Media Power after the Cold War." In *Decisionmaking in a Glass House: Mass Media, Public Opinion, and American and European Foreign Policy in the 21st Century,* edited by Brigitte L. Nacos, Robert Y. Shapiro, and Pierangelo Isernia, 11–26. Lanham, MD: Rowman & Littlefield, 2000.

———. "Reporting Environmental Policy Debate: The Real Media Bias." *Harvard International Journal of Press/Politics* 1, no. 3 (1996): 77–92.

Entman, Robert M., and Andrew Rojecki. *The Black Image in the White Mind*. Chicago: University of Chicago Press, 2000.

Gans, Herbert J. *Deciding What's News*. New York: Vintage Books, 1979.

Gilens, Martin. "Race and Poverty in America: Public Misperceptions and the American News Media." *Public Opinion Quarterly* 60, no. 4 (1996): 515–41.

———. *Why Americans Hate Welfare: Race, Media, and the Politics of Antipoverty Policy*. Chicago: University of Chicago Press, 1999.

Gissler, Sig. "Newspapers Quest for Racial Candor." *Media Studies Journal* 8, no. 3 (1994): 123–32.

Gitlin, Todd. *The Whole World is Watching.* Berkeley: University of California Press, 1980.

Graber, Doris. "Seeing is Remembering: How Visuals Contribute to Learning from Television News." *Journal of Communication* 40, no. 3 (1997): 134–55.

Heymann, Philip B. *Terrorism, Freedom, and Security: Winning Without War.* Cambridge, MA: MIT Press, 2003.

Huddy, Leonie et al. "Fear and Terrorism: Psychological Reactions to 9/11." In *Framing Terrorism: The News Media, the Government, and the Public,* edited by Pippa Norri, Montague Kern, and Marion Just, 255–78. New York: Routledge, 2003.

Iyengar, Shanto. *Is Anyone Responsible?* Chicago: University of Chicago Press, 1991.

Kern, Montague. "The Invasion of Afghanistan: Domestic vs. Foreign Stories." In *Television Coverage of the Middle East,* edited by William C. Adams, 106–27. Norwood, NJ: Ablex Publishing, 1981.

Kinder, Donald R., and Lynn Sanders. *Divided by Color: Racial Politics and Democratic Ideals.* Chicago: University of Chicago Press, 1996.

Lippmann, Walter. *Public Opinion.* New York: Free Press, 1997. First published in 1922.

Nacos, Brigitte L. *Mass-Mediated Terrorism: The Central Role of the Media in Terrorism and Counterterrorism.* Lanham, MD: Rowman & Littlefield, 2002.

———. *The Press, Presidents, and Crises.* New York: Columbia University Press, 1990.

Nacos, Brigitte L., and Oscar Torres-Reyna. "Framing Muslim-Americans before and after 9/11." In *Framing Terrorism: The News Media, the Government, and the Public,* edited by Pippa Norris, Montague Kern, and Marion Just, 133–57. New York: Routledge, 2003.

Nacos, Brigitte, and Natasha Hritzuk. "The Portrayal of Black America in the Mass Media." In *Black and Multicultural Politics in America,* edited by M. Alex Assensoh and Lawrence Hanks, 165–195. New York: New York University Press, 2000.

National Commission on Civil Disorders, *Report of the National Commission on Civil Disorders.* New York: The New York Times Company, 1968.

Neumann, Russel W., Marion Just, and Ann N. Crigler. *Common Knowledge: News and the Construction of Political Meaning.* Chicago: University of Chicago Press, 1992.

Nisbet, Erik C., and James Shanahan. "Restrictions on Civil Liberties, Views of Islam & Muslim Americans." Media and Society Group, Cornell University, December 2004.

Noelle-Neumann, Elisabeth. *The Spiral of Silence: Public Opinion—Our Social Skin.* Chicago: University of Chicago Press, 1984.

Norris, Pippa. *Women, Media, and Politics.* New York: Oxford University Press, 1997.

Said, Edward W. *Covering Islam: How the Media and the Experts Determine how we see the Rest of the World.* New York: Pantheon Books, 1981.

Shaheen, Jack. *Arab and Muslim Stereotypes in American Popular Culture.* Washington, DC: Center for Muslim-Christian Understanding, 1997.

———. *Reel Bad Arabs: How Hollywood Vilifies a People.* Northampton, MA: Interlink Publishing Group, 2001.

Shanahan, James, and Michael Morgan. *Television and Its Viewers: Cultivation Theory and Research.* New York: Cambridge University Press, 1999.

Shipler, David K. "Blacks in the Newsrooms. Progress? Yes, but . . ." *Columbia Journalism Review* (May/June 1998): 26–32.

Simon, Reeva. *The Middle East in Crime Fiction*. New York: Lilian Barber Press, 1989.

Sprinzak, Ehud. "The psychopolitical formation of extreme left terrorism in a democracy: The case of the Weathermen." In *Origins of Terrorism: Psychologies, Ideologies, Theologies, States of Mind*, edited by Walter Reich, 64–85. New York: Cambridge University Press, 1990.

Index

Page numbers in italics refer to tables.

About the Authors

Brigitte L. Nacos is adjunct professor of political science at Columbia University. She is the author of several books, among them *Terrorism and Counterterrorism: Threats and Responses in the Post-9/11 World* (2006), *Mass-Mediated Terrorism* (2002), *Decisionmaking in a Glass House* (2000, with Robert Y. Shapiro and Pierangelo Isernia), *Terrorism and the Media: From the Iran Hostage Crisis to the Oklahoma City Bombing* (1996), and *The Press, Presidents, and Crises* (1990). Her blog is reflectivepundit (www.reflectivepundit.com).

Oscar Torres-Reyna is a PhD candidate in political science at Columbia University. He worked in the president of Mexico's polling unit from 1990 to 1996, participated in several research projects at Columbia University, and co-authored articles in *Public Opinion Quarterly*. He is currently a visiting professor of public policy at Universidad de Guadalajara in Mexico.